Alone in Marriage

ENCOURAGEMENT FOR THE TIMES
WHEN IT'S ALL UP TO YOU

Alone in Marriage

SUSIE LARSON

MOODY PUBLISHERS
Chicago

Unless otherwise indicated, all Scripture quotations are taken from the *Holy Bible, New Living Translation*, copyright © 1996, 2004. Used by permission of Tyndale House Publishers, Inc., Wheaton Illinois 60189, U.S.A. All rights reserved.

Scripture quotations marked NLT are taken from the *Holy Bible, New Living Translation*, copyright © 1996. Used by permission of Tyndale House Publishers, Inc., Wheaton Illinois 60189, U.S.A. All rights reserved.

Scripture quotations marked NIV are taken from the *Holy Bible, New International Version*®. NIV®. Copyright © 1973, 1978, 1984 by International Bible Society. Used by permission of Zondervan. All rights reserved.

Scripture quotations marked THE MESSAGE are from *The Message*, copyright © by Eugene H. Peterson 1993, 1994, 1995. Used by permission of NavPress Publishing Group.

Scripture quotations marked HCSB are taken from the Holman Christian Standard Bible®, Copyright © 1999, 2000, 2002, 2003 by Holman Bible Publishers. Used by permission. Holman Christian Standard Bible®, Holman CSB®, and HCSB® are federally registered trademarks of Holman Bible Publishers.

Scripture quotations marked NASB are taken from the *New American Standard Bible*®, Copyright © 1960, 1962, 1963, 1968, 1971, 1972, 1973, 1975, 1977, 1995 by The Lockman Foundation. Used by permission. (www.Lockman.org)

Editor: Pam Pugh
Published in association with the literary agency of Alive Communications, Inc., 7680 Goddard Street, Suite 200, Colorado Springs, CO 80920. (www.alivecommunications.com)

Library of Congress Cataloging-in-Publication Data

Larson, Susie, 1962-
  Alone in marriage : encouragement for the times when it's all up to you / Susie Larson.
      p. cm.
  Includes bibliographical references.
  ISBN-10: 0-8024-5278-7
  ISBN-13: 978-0-8024-5278-8
  1. Wives--Religious life. 2. Christian women--Religious life. 3. Marriage--Religious aspects--Christianity. I. Title.
  BV4528.15.L37 2007
  248.8'435--dc22
                              2007007605

All emphases in Scripture citations are the author's. Real-life narratives throughout the book are all true, although names and certain details may have been changed.

We hope you enjoy this book from Moody Publishers. Our goal is to provide high-quality, thought-provoking books and products that connect truth to your real needs and challenges. For more information on other books and products written and produced from a biblical perspective, go to www.moodypublishers.com or write to:

Moody Publishers
820 N. LaSalle Boulevard
Chicago, IL 60610

5 7 9 10 8 6 4

Printed in the United States of America

To my girlfriend Daryl Jackson
I've learned a lot about love by watching you.
I love you, friend.

To my precious Mom, Pat Erickson
Your love and endurance have challenged me to climb.
I love you, Mom.

To my faithful husband, Kevin
You've had to carry me more miles than I've carried you.
You are my best friend. Thanks for letting me write this book.
I love you, honey.

To my Beloved, Jesus
You show me every day what it means to be Yours.
I love You most.

CONTENTS

WHAT THIS
BOOK IS ABOUT

WHEN YOU first said "I do," did you have any idea it would be like this? Are you currently carrying more than you bargained for?

Everyone who marries will eventually encounter a season or two where the weight of the relationship is on their shoulders. Spouses get sick, distracted, selfish, or overworked; they pursue further education or start new businesses; they live a lie, or stop believing, they overcommit or overspend. Life happens, the weight shifts, and suddenly we find ourselves wondering, "Is this how God meant it to be?"

Women are not the only ones who end up carrying the weight of the marriage on their shoulders. Countless heroic men have held the home together while their wives were sick or distracted or somewhere else. My husband is one of those men, and you'll read his story in the last chapter. But this book is for women because I am a woman and I speak to women. I also know what it is to carry more of my marriage than I bargained for. Also, after interviewing many women, I have a better understanding of what kinds of feelings, struggles, and questions come up during such seasons.

My prayer is that this book will nourish your soul as you walk through your own season. My purpose isn't to improve your marriage or even change your spouse. If you are a woman of faith and you are in a season of marriage that feels especially heavy, this book is for you. You can be a strong Christian and be in a strong marriage, and still endure a one-sided season.

If you want more from God and want your capacity for God to increase amidst a trying time, you've come to the right place. This book addresses the Christian woman's spiritual journey through a heavy season in marriage. This book is to encourage, challenge, and bless *you*. And yet as your soul gets nourished and your love matures, your marriage will also be improved and blessed.

The book is divided into three sections. The first section will address the unnecessary weights we carry like anger, worry, fear, and self-pity. The second section will explore the weights that refine us—disappointment, loneliness, imperfection, and waiting. The third and final section explores what is available for those who believe. As your prayers, perspective, and words line up with God's Word, you will be inspired to possess your land of promise. When faith, hope, and love are present, thriving in every season—even the alone times—becomes a possibility.

Throughout each chapter you'll find stories from Christian women (and one from my husband) who have endured their own seasons of struggle and triumph. From situations with husbands who are simply overworked and overcommitted or got sick, to ones who are depressed, out of work, in a midlife crisis, or away from home for an extended period, these stories will help you to know that you are not alone and that no circumstance can keep you from becoming all God wants you to be. You were called to

□

be holy and confident, secure and fruitful, and no matter where life finds you, these things are possible for you.

May the Lord Jesus, under whose shelter you have come for protection, bless you as you read.

—SUSIE LARSON

Section One

WEIGHTS THAT WEAR YOU DOWN

1. ANGER

2. WORRY

3. FEAR

4. SELF-PITY

One

ANGER

Put on your new nature, created to be like God—
truly righteous and holy. And "don't sin by
letting anger control you."

Don't let the sun go down while you are still angry,
for anger gives a foothold to the devil.

Ephesians 4:24, 26–27

I COULD feel my love growing cold. I hated how I felt inside, and yet everything in me wanted to build a wall around my heart so there would be no more hopes or expectations to fall dead at my feet. But a walled-off heart makes for a heavy load. Eventually, your legs give out from under you.

Being a woman of God, I spent a lot of time every morning in Scripture and in prayer; I loved to worship God and serve in my church. I had an active walk of faith and yet the honest truth was that my love for my husband was fading, and I was only dragging my feet down the path of duty.

How could I reconcile loving God but not my husband? I couldn't. As a child of God, I knew I could not compartmentalize such things and get away with it for very long. Gradually, my attitude toward my husband spilled over into other areas of my life. Little things irritated me more than they should. I assumed certain people had malicious motives when they probably didn't. And worst of all, God's voice grew more and more quiet with each passing day.

God wasn't moving away from me, of course, but I was moving away from Him. We know we can't have it both ways. We can't love God and dislike people. The *Peanuts* character Linus once said, "I love mankind—it's people I can't stand!" That sentiment may be humorous, but God won't let us off with such a conclusion. Jesus declared the most important commandment to be that we love God with everything in us. He continued by saying, "A second is *equally* important: 'Love your neighbor as yourself'" (Matthew 22:39).

Through the early years of our marriage, we dealt with many trials—health issues being the greatest—and because we had poor insurance, we found ourselves in deep financial debt. Amidst all of this my husband was a rock and worked hard, sometimes two or three jobs to keep us afloat.

Eventually though, our long season of back-to-back crises subsided, and we began the hard work of rebuilding our lives. Over the years, we paid back more than twenty thousand dollars worth of medical debt. Day after day, month after month, year after year, we applied ourselves to getting on our feet again.

Some days we felt weary and worn out and wondered if we were making any forward progress at all. But always at the right time, God mercifully encouraged us onward. He even put it in the hearts of a couple of our debtors to forgive our debts. Several times we received gifts from loving friends. We also worked hard and saved enough to build a new home and start fresh. All of this

☐

took time, but it was well worth the effort. That season was so painful it took years before I could look back on those memories without getting a pit in my stomach.

God faithfully led us through the wilderness. *And yet*, even though time had passed and life was better for us, and even though we were no longer in crisis mode, my husband worked as though we were. He became a true-blue workaholic.

Life became a blur as Kevin raced through life. I knew there was no way to get that time back. As my husband spent more and more time at work, he left more and more undone at home. The ripple effect of his choices created waves of anxiety that continually stirred within me.

Several times throughout our married life, Kevin faced the truth that he tended to trust himself more than God. Upon each revelation, he felt sincerely sorry and determined to live a more balanced life that included time to manage our home life and time with the family. And yet eventually these seasons always passed, and Kevin was back to racing through life like a freight train.

A time came when our church needed someone to head up the building program. Kevin took on that role on top of his forty- to fifty-hour day job. He was excited about the prospect of serving God in a big way, and this role fit his talents perfectly.

Kevin jumped in with both feet, and within no time, things shifted and our marriage went way out of balance. There was no room in our already crowded marriage for a twenty- to twenty-five-hour a week commitment. We had three sons; I was working part-time as an aerobics instructor, and speaking occasionally at retreats and conferences, all the while trying to keep the dishes, the laundry, and the housework done; and together we were overseeing the youth program at our church (crazy, I know). I must confess this is a very humbling story for us to share.

Kevin was all but absent from home. And when he was home, he was on the phone, working on the computer, or buried in blueprints. The kids and I talked to the side of his face while he opened the mail. Still, when we did get his attention, he was the sweetest and kindest guy in the world.

In his defense, he really felt inspired that he was doing something worthwhile. In his day job, he oversees large construction projects. So to volunteer time overseeing the building of a church was very meaningful to him. And once the job grew before our eyes, he felt he could not abandon his post. People were depending on him, and the excitement was building (no pun intended). I felt that he chose the building over me. Not that I wanted him to quit or walk away from the project; I just wanted him to invest *some* time into the things he was neglecting at home.

I worked hard to keep a good attitude, especially in front of the kids, but since there were little to no emotional deposits being made into our marriage for months at a time, our relationship was steadily going bankrupt. Slowly but surely, my disappointment turned to anger that eventually turned to cold love.

One day while crying out to God and begging Him to intervene, He spoke very clearly to my heart. *Susie, I know Kevin is overcommitted and missing it right now, but you are the one who has committed the greater sin. Though Kevin's priorities are off and need some adjusting, he is still very much in love with you and the boys. You've committed the worse offense, because you've allowed your love to grow cold. I want you to go sit at his feet and apologize for this sin and ask him for forgiveness. If you want to fulfill all of the wonderful things I've called you to, you will walk in humble forgiveness all of the days of your life.*

I was aghast. I thought back to countless conversations, trying to get through to Kevin, and all I could see was a blank stare that told me, *I won't change my schedule until this project is done.* So to go to him and apologize seemed like the most vulnerable, unfair thing to do. If anything, my anger had become my friend. I had let go of the hope of him changing, and my anger *fueled* me to get done what needed to get done.

But I love and fear the Lord and have surrendered my life to Him. He always deserves my obedience. As I spent more time pondering how my love had grown cold, I thought of the countless selfish acts I had committed. I gave Kevin the small piece of chicken, the bumpy pillow, and sometimes I would go to bed without saying good night. I stopped thinking his jokes were funny and I lost my desire to dream with him. Not only, I am sure, had I hurt my husband, but my lack of love was a direct affront to my gracious and merciful God.

I did not want to live with anger! But to go and lay it down at the feet of my husband with no hope or promise that he would see what it cost me seemed almost over my head. I prayed for several days for my own selfish heart—that God would prepare me in all sincerity—and that God would prepare my husband as well.

After dinner one night I went into the living room where Kevin was looking at his notes from a recent meeting. I swallowed hard and sat on the floor by his feet. I looked up at him and he looked right into my eyes. He put his notes down as if he knew I had something important to say.

I opened my mouth to say my first word and my eyes filled with tears. I proceeded. "I need to ask your forgiveness for something. You know I've been very hurt and angry over how things have gone these past two years. Well, the Lord showed me that between the two of us, I am the one who has committed the greater offense; I've allowed my love to grow cold. Please forgive me. Though my feelings toward you have changed, I am going to make a conscious effort to love and serve you whether you understand me or not. I want all of what God has for me and I am going to do what He asks me to do."

As I spoke, Kevin's mouth dropped open. It was as if with each word I spoke, another scale fell from his eyes. After I finished, his voice cracked and he asked, "Is *this* what my choices have been doing to you?" I put my face in my hands and wept. It was like a dam broke and I couldn't stop it. Kevin came down on the floor and wrapped me in his arms. There we sat, on the same level, two very imperfect people, desperately in need of God's fresh mercies and grace.

From that day forward I kept my word and made the conscious effort to love my husband while he struggled to overcome his workaholic tendencies. And to be honest, there were days when love was simply a choice. Over time, though, we were able to share our deep-seated fears and disappointments. Little by little we made deposits in an account that had been emptied. We now put strict boundaries around our time and we tenaciously guard our date nights.

Years have passed and I can honestly say that when I look at my husband, I find love in my heart that almost overwhelms me. He is funny and strong and faithful. He has worked hard to make choices that have covered our home and rebuilt my trust. I see God actively working in him, and he sees God actively working in me.

Now please let me say that every situation is different (and complex) in its own way and obedience looks different on everyone. In some situations anger is an appropriate response. At that

□

moment in the living room, obedience for me was to bow low; for you at this moment, to obey may be to stand strong.[1] Even so, for all of us, the outcome is in God's hands.

I have the opportunity to speak to countless women and my heart just breaks every time I hear a new story of pain and frustration. Their tired eyes reveal the burden and the load they are carrying.

Jane is dealing with her husband's addiction to pornography. Melanie is watching her husband's obsession with computer games eat up all of their family time. Julie takes life a day at a time as her husband goes from one consuming hobby to another.

Please remember that you are not alone. Many women feel what you feel and long for the same sense of joy and freedom in their lives that you do. Take a few steps within your own sphere of influence and you'll find other women carrying a burden they hadn't planned on carrying.

Some are dealing with the wretched pain of infidelity and wonder how they will ever trust anyone again. Others are dealing with the drain of living with someone bound by an addiction.

Many women deal with the constant anxiety of being married to a spouse who cannot keep a job; others ride the roller coaster of living with a loved one who struggles with depression. Some have learned to walk on eggshells because of their spouse's obsessions. Others wish their spouses would notice *something* and snap out of their apathy.

Moving day should have been a clue. I stood on the steps of our new home with a three-month-old on my hip and an inquisitive three-year-old darting around moving men and boxes. My husband was not there; he was on call. I did not know my neighbors and no family members lived nearby. I felt very alone.

Relocating five states away for my husband's medical residency seemed like a good idea. We chose our program carefully, looking for one with low call the first year. "One night a week" was the description. The actual program did not fit the description, and he had a call schedule of one in every three nights. My husband was gone one night, sleeping the next, and present but grumpy on the third night. I often described this year as feeling that I had a live-in boyfriend rather than a husband. He showed up randomly and did not participate in home life, parenting, or church hunting.

After fifteen months, I began sliding into a deep depression. My attempts at talking to my husband were not received well. He worked over eighty hours a week and just wanted me to "get it together." He did not have the time or emotional resources to handle my problems. I had no close friends or older women in whom I could confide. I did not spend time in prayer or Bible study. I waited for all of my needs to be met by my very busy husband.

The emotional stress mounted until I suffered a complete breakdown. When I was encouraged to enter a hospital for treatment, my husband and I settled on a different plan. He took a leave of absence from work and we began counseling together.

My husband realized that a career was not worth losing a wife and children. He committed to making family a priority. I admitted that I needed to look to God to meet my emotional and spiritual needs rather than to my husband. No man can fill the needs intended to be met by God.

> Stressful times magnify what is in a marriage—or better or
> worse. Our crisis revealed the worst, and we chose to let God
> change us. My husband now has the compassion and
> understanding to treat depressed patients in his family practice. I
> teach women's Bible studies and look for young mothers who
> need mentoring as I did, and because of my experiences, I'm able
> to direct them to God and His Word to meet their needs.
>
> —Emma from Texas

Some wives deal with the stress of having a materialistic, per-
fectionist for a spouse; they are in debt up to their eyeballs and
would give anything for a simpler, free life. Other wives are worn
out from living with husbands who are messy pack rats and only
dream about having a sense of order in the home. All of these im-
balances create a burden for the spouse, and anger is a natural by-
product when these kinds of stresses occur.

And yet as real as these struggles are and as hopeless as things
sometimes feel, even more real and steadfast is this promise: God
will *never* forsake His own; and we are His own. Our spouses may
get caught up in many things that will directly affect our lives.
They may make choices that devastate us. We may feel completely
misunderstood at times. But we must not despair because God understands and He has made a way for us.

⸺

Are you carrying weights that drag you down? Is one of them
anger? If you are angry, it's possible you have a good reason. You
may feel especially entitled to your anger. But do you know how
dangerous unresolved anger can be? Is anger worth having along
when you know it gives the Devil easy access to your life? Please

SPIRITUAL LIFT:

"Underneath our every step are God's everlasting arms. Thus, when we pass through spiritual conflicts and trials, we are walking on eternal ground, continually kept by the power of Christ's indestructible life."

Francis Frangipane[2]

know that he wants to blow up and injure everything and everyone around you.

Anger can make us cold; it can make us hot; it can take us off the path, or it can blow our path to smithereens. Anger is natural, but it needs to be disarmed. Would you dare pack explosives before going to an airport? Packing anger in your spiritual luggage is just as dangerous. It's easily detected, sets off alarms, and puts people on the defensive.

Underneath our anger is a certain mistrust of God. Somewhere along the way we stopped believing that God is a God of love and of justice. If we truly believed that our lives, our hopes, and our dreams were in God's hands, we wouldn't be quite so shocked when imperfect people hurt us or let us down.

We can thrive in these desperate places! It is much too easy to think, "If only my life (or husband) was different, *then* I wouldn't be so angry and I would finally find the joy I am looking for . . . " or "*then* I would be more productive," or "*then* I would be a better person." And yet, it is on *this* journey that we find all of the things we are looking for and find God to be all of who He says He is.

I say this with great care, but our ultimate goal is not our happiness or even getting our way; our goal is the high calling of becoming more like Christ. Instead of fighting for a perfect life, we surrender to God that we might be perfected. Instead of being angry that life has scraped us, we allow the rough times to shape us into the image of Christ.

When we understand that it's *this* journey that will deepen us, we will find a joy that trumps the world's fleeting happiness, entitlements, and shallow selfishness, every time.

Though we may feel otherwise, anger is not our friend. Anger will betray us if we insist on coddling, nurturing, and protecting our right to it. And there will be countless reasons to get very angry over the course of our married lives. We will be overlooked, taken advantage of, and treated rudely. Our spouses are imperfect people. Unfortunately our spouses are married to women who need Jesus' refining in our lives just as badly as they do.

What do we do, though, when the anger rises up within us? How do we keep an eternal perspective when the moment is pierced with pain? The Bible says, "In your anger do not sin; when you are on your beds, search your hearts and be silent" (Psalm 4:4 NIV).

Let's take a closer look at what this passage means for us:

How often when wounded by someone else's sin, do *we* sin by our response to them? More than once I've told my boys that the Christian life is like a winding country road with deep ditches on each side. One side represents outright rebellion, the other *our response* to someone else's rebellion. The Devil couldn't care less which ditch he gets us into; he just wants us off the road.

Is your husband rebelling against God and sinning by his self-ishness? Don't allow your anger or self-righteousness over his sin to catapult you into the other ditch. Again, Satan doesn't care if you're in the ditch because of rebellion or a false sense of perfection; he just wants you off the road. These are moments of truth for us, and our choices are critical. When we are wronged, let's not allow our anger to betray us or forfeit what God has for us! May we always have the courage to let God deal with those who make us angry and dare to pray, "Search *me*, O God, and know *my heart*; test me and know *my anxious thoughts*. Point out anything in *me* that offends *you*, and lead *me* along the path of everlasting life" (Psalm 139:23–24).

In my book *Balance That Works When Life Doesn't*, I wrote about how heavy things can make us stronger. Later in this book, we will explore how certain heavy struggles can refine and strengthen us. But for now it is important to know and remember that anger is *not* a weight that will contribute to our growth. Traveling with anger as our companion will only serve to weaken us and diminish our ability to know and share God's love. "People with understanding control their anger; a hot temper shows great foolishness" (Proverbs 14:29).

LENDING A HAND

Watch Your Step—Be careful not to think of yourself as a victim unless you truly are—in which case; don't wait; get the help you need! In every situation, God's love can reach you and will provide a way for you. Refuse to allow anger to become an explosive force in your life. Do not dwell on your anger toward your husband—repent of it. As legitimate as your anger may be, it will betray and eventually destroy you. Ask God to take your anger from you. He will respond. In due time, He will intervene.

Get on the Right Path—Remember to think of yourself as an overcomer. Remember that God is a God of justice, and He will defend the humble heart. Remember to search your own heart. Remember that God is big enough to do something beautiful in your marriage.

Run From—Run from conversations that stir up your anger. Guard your speech and only talk about your situation with friends who walk in the humble fear of the Lord. Rehearsing and revisiting offenses only re-offends the soul and re-injures the relationship. Run from a complaining, grumbling attitude and embrace hopeful expectation instead.

Destination Ahead—Run toward the Word of God, toward times in His presence, and toward people who love you and call you to higher ground. Rather than go through the motions of being the good Christian wife while anger overtakes your inner life, get real with God. Give Him every detail of every emotion you are feeling. Stay connected with your church family. Keep your prayer life alive.

Watch the Fine Line—Guard your heart from anger, humble yourself before God, and be willing to forgive. BUT don't confuse this humble posture with being a doormat, someone who never expresses your thoughts and disappointments, and who misguidedly thinks it noble and martyrlike to let others walk all over you.

God's Promise for You Today—"In his kindness God called you to share in his eternal glory by means of Christ Jesus. After you have suffered a little while, he will restore, support, and strengthen you, and he will place you on a firm foundation" (1 Peter 5:10).

Precious Lord,

Help me to keep my heart pure. I long to walk in Your presence as I live here on earth (Psalm 116:9). You know what has broken my heart and You know what it will take to heal me. Heal me, Lord! And restore me! Fill me up with a heart of love and forgiveness for my husband. Help me to see him as You do. It doesn't matter if he is not seeing things clearly; You do, and that's what counts. I entrust myself into Your care, knowing You will come through for me in time. Keep anger from betraying me so I can be faithful to You and those I love. I need You every hour. Amen.

TO THINK ABOUT...

1. Read Ephesians 4:26–27

Allowing our anger to take hold of us (and our perspective) is not only a sin; it gives the Devil a mighty foothold. Describe a time when you regretfully allowed anger to poison your life.

What would you do differently today?

The Greek word for the term "foothold" in this passage is *topos*, which means opportunity, occasion, power, space, and place. When we give way to our anger, we give the Devil ample opportunity, power, and occasion to ruin our lives. Does this make you look at anger differently? If so, explain. If not, explain.

2. Read Matthew 6:14–15

a. How does this passage make you feel?

b. Look out the window. Imagine if you had a cross planted in your yard and nailed to it was a list of offenses for your neighbors to see. When you look at the cross, do you see a list of your husband's misdeeds, or is your own list the first thing you see? Or do you walk in such a day-to-day fellowship with God that when you look at the empty cross you are simply thankful?

c. Though most of us don't have a cross in our front yards, we do display the offenses committed against us and by us in the way we walk and talk and live. When we walk closely with the Lord, our lists are quickly reconciled with Christ's forgiveness and only the evidence of His love remains. Do you have a list that needs to be covered in the mercy of Christ? Do you need to forgive yourself and/or your husband? Write down what comes to mind. Take the time, do the work, get rid of your lists, and walk in forgiveness!

3. Read Ephesians 4:30–32

a. Take a minute and write this passage out in a personalized prayer. Maybe this will help you get started: "Precious Father, May I never bring You sorrow by the way that I live because I belong to You. You've identified me as Your own. . . . "

b. Now for something a little different—I call this a "listening prayer." Write a love letter to yourself from

Jesus; what do you suppose Jesus wants to say to you during this season? I will give you a running start: "My precious child, I love you so. I know what makes your heart break, but I want you to know . . . "*

4. Determine not to neglect your regular times of reading and prayer. When anger rises up, bow low and entrust yourself to God. Identify something in your life that has the potential to pull you away from your relationship to God and write it down. Pause for a moment and ask the Lord for wisdom in this matter. Write down what you sense He is telling you.

*This is a prayer exercise and what you write should not be taken as gospel (i.e., "God told me . . . "), or replace what you read in the Bible. The more acquainted you are with Scripture and the heart of the Father, the more biblically accurate your listening prayers will become. Even so, we only know in part; and yet God loves to reveal Himself to those who seek after Him.

Two

WORRY

Don't worry about anything; instead, pray about everything.
Tell God what you need, and thank him for all he has done.

□ Philippians 4:6

MY JOURNEY had been a long one. I arrived home from the airport ready to drop, in deep need of rest. I sank right into bed like a dead weight and fell fast asleep. When I woke up the next day, I began to unpack my bags. Item by item, I removed my things and put them away. As I lifted up my Ziploc bag of lotions and creams, I cringed. I thought I had twisted the cap of hand lotion on tight, but apparently not. The goopy lotion filled the bag and smothered all of my other bottles. Thankfully I had had the presence of mind to use Ziploc.

Worry, like oozing lotion, doesn't like to stay in one place. Seasons change, the pressure builds, and before we know it, worry overtakes every area of our lives (creating a mess that's difficult to clean up). Worry blurs the lines between actual trials and potential problems, making it difficult to know where one ends and the other begins. Worry overtakes our perspective and drains us of strength, peace, and joy.

Worry makes life messy.

What do you worry most about? Is it finances, your children, your health, your husband's choices? I've worried about all these things, and I have yet to meet anyone who lives a completely worry-free life. Loved ones die, spouses get distracted, finances dry up, friends go away, and suddenly we find ourselves feeling like the weight of the world is on our shoulders. The truth is, there *is* much to worry about! When stresses are heaped upon us and the pressure of life boils over, our capacity for worry increases as well.

It is especially during the "one-sided" seasons in marriage that we are at risk of losing perspective and gaining the weight of worry. I learned a lot about refusing to be overwhelmed by worry as I walked with a friend who carried a load that would have crushed me. She loved and cared for her husband who was sick, and she received very little in return. She was the one who had the full-time job, brought home the money, and paid the bills. She kept the house clean. She did the yard work. She cared for the children. She prayed for things to change. She was lonely. She was overlooked. And she got overwhelmed at times.

Whether she was tired and crabby, or hanging on by a thread of hope, God gave me the privilege of seeing her through His eyes. What I saw when I looked at her was an enormous amount of character, integrity, and class. I felt such an intense amount of love and respect for her, and I knew that God was proud of her.

Some days she would fall apart, wondering how she would ever find the strength to continue. But somewhere in the midst of these despairing moments, she would bring herself back to the Word and remind herself who she was to God. I could always tell when she had been with God because her eyes sparkled with a fresh filling of peace and trust. She refused to allow worry to weigh her down or mark her life.

You might be in the toughest part of your season and be too tired to pray. That's okay. Ask your friends and family to pray for you, and trust that their prayers will make a difference. Determine to dwell longer on God than you do your circumstances. In order to do more than merely survive these trying times, our eyes need to be fixed on Him. Our circumstances may be screaming at us, and it seems God only whispers at times, yet leaning in and listening to Him will calm our hearts, and looking to Him will bring us peace in place of worry. Fears of what could happen are as countless as the sands on the seashore, and though *some* things we fear might happen, most of them never will. Even so, we cannot live our lives floating down the river of denial hoping that no low-hanging branch will ever knock us out of our boat. No, we have to be alert and aware of potential dangers, and we have to acknowledge stresses as they come, but somehow we are called to do this without being overcome by worry.

We cannot control everything that comes our way in marriage, but believe it or not, *we* are the ones who decide if our lives are marked by worry or by a patient trust in a heavenly Father who loves us and knows where we are at every minute.

We are given just enough grace, mercy, and provision for the road we are on, because that's all we can handle. While it is true that God allows us to walk through unimaginable times of difficulty, we are never out of His care, and there is a limit to each and every struggle we face.

We are especially prone to worry when several areas of our lives feel under pressure or out of balance. If our marriage is strained and finances are tight and we're snapping at the kids as a result, the ripple effect can tie us up in knots. After all, we only have two hands, right? Thankfully, having two hands has very little to do with our capacity to carry multiple problems at a time without the presence of worry. We have to work hard at walking in faith and refusing worry. Daily, we must proclaim, "I will not carry worry with me today—not any day. Jesus calls me to peace!"

As we reflect on our God, the One who gave us breath and life and promised to care for us, we become more assured of the magnitude of His strength and less intimidated by the size of our problems. When we remember that the hairs on our head are numbered and that the birds outside our window are under the Lord's watchful eye, our hearts will rest secure. Such assurance of the Father's love makes my knees weak. I aspire to walk in this assurance on a more regular basis.

It is possible to walk through stress or injustice in the absence of worry. But it takes an intentional pursuit of peace.

Peace can be found in even the most tragic of circumstances. But peace is quenched when worry is given free rein. It starts in the mind. First we entertain questions that all begin with "what if" until the worst-case scenarios catch our attention and take residence in our minds. Soon our mulled-over thoughts become full-blown worries spilling over onto our already-heavy burden. It doesn't matter if most of our worries won't come to fruition and ruin our lives; just worrying about them does that for us.

In her wonderful book *Calm My Anxious Heart*, Linda Dillow writes,

Modern medical research has proven that worry breaks down resistance to disease. More than that, it actually diseases the nervous system, and particularly affects the digestive organs and the heart. When we add to this the toll of sleepless nights and days void of contentment, we glimpse the stranglehold worry has on the human heart. Worry doesn't empty tomorrow of its sorrow, it empties today of its strength.[1]

I know you have some legitimate worries right now. I know what it is to look at your situation and wonder if anyone understands the stress of your season. Know this: You are not alone—not by a long stretch. In fact, when you live for and trust in the Lord, you must remember that far greater is He who is for you than those who are against you! Instead of brooding over your concerns, dwell on the fact that you are loved and adored by your heavenly Bridegroom.

Your husband may be in a season of distraction or destruction. He may seem far away or be so clingy that you are constantly tripping over him. You may feel the longing to have him home at night, or the desperate need for some breathing room. No matter what changes have taken place in your husband, God *never* changes and He's not going anywhere. He is by your side and wants to be intimately involved with all that concerns you.

It had never been my desire to manage the family finances. But as it turned out, that became my role to handle alone.

Pete and I both had jobs, but he would write checks and spend money on things that were not budgeted, and this money would even be spent before bills were paid. He "forgot" to mention his purchases, and I sometimes didn't find out about them until I'd write a check at a store, only to be told that it was declined due to insufficient funds! I tried to get him to take a class in managing personal finances, but he refused. This all led to major anxiety for me.

I started to stash away money where he couldn't find out about it.

I was brought up to tithe and wanted to do so, but Pete was distrustful of pastors because he knew about some situations of financial misuse. Our lack of giving led to more anxiety and loneliness for me. Since I didn't believe in sharing our problems with anyone, I internalized my feelings until I was filled with resentment, bitterness, frustration, and anger. I finally gave up on him sharing the load of being responsible and writing out the bills, and did it all myself.

This aspect of our lives was a major source of contention for many years. Finally one day he was frustrated because he said I was controlling him by limiting his overspending, so I angrily gave him the checkbook and told him fine—he was welcome to take over the finances completely.

I realized I needed to be free from the bitterness, anger, anxiety, and resentment. I asked God to work in me and take them away.

To my surprise, one night at Bible study, Pete stood in the pulpit and publicly confessed and apologized to me in front of the congregation for making our finances such a burden for me. I was shocked and a little embarrassed. I had no idea what prompted him to do that. Then he asked me to come up to the podium and to publicly forgive him. I was nearly speechless, but I did it. All I could think was, *What a guy!*

He's since taken an accounting class, met with a financial planner, and written a vision statement for himself. God has worked in both of us, and now we are committed tithers. My

anxious days in money management are gone and I am free!
—Dorothy from Los Angeles

Whatever causes your heart to worry, may you only look at it long enough to bring it to God and leave it there. Then, place your heart, your future, and your husband in His hands and take one step at a time into the future. He will faithfully lead you. Rest assured, He will.

It is okay if your knees are wobbling and your heart is racing when facing your fears and concerns. A trembling heart entrusted to God is very dear to Him; He will handle it with the utmost care. Refusing worry is never about having it all together, but about knowing that we *don't*, and yielding ourselves to the One who does.

SPIRITUAL LIFT:

"Lift your heart and let it rest upon Jesus and you are instantly in a sanctuary. . . . You can see God from anywhere if your mind is set to love and obey Him."

☐ *A. W. Tozer*[2]

When worry is uncontained, it overtakes our precious time. Have you ever thought about how much *time* we spend worrying? I can think of countless wasted moments when my eyes glazed over as I stared out the window, wondering when Kevin would find balance. I was so worried about my husband missing sacred moments; I missed many of them myself.

And yet whenever I took the time to take my thoughts captive and make them obedient to Christ (read 2 Corinthians 10:5), I found moments of clarity, peace, and even motivation to do something about my circumstances.

TAKE INITIATIVE!

Taking initiative puts worry back in its place. In every situation there is something we can do, because no situation is outside of God's care for us; and in every situation, He has made a way for us. You've said to yourself over and over again, "I wish there was something I could do, but there is nothing." That is never true. You can pray, you can fast, you can rest, you can use the time to get to know God better, you can work, you can spend more time with your kids, you can organize your bills, and you can take better care of yourself.

Find passages of Scripture that are helpful to you, such as Matthew 6:25–33 and 10:29–31.

Pray and read the following passage out loud. See what other helpful verses you can find.

"Even though the fig trees have no blossoms, and there are no grapes on the vines; even though the olive crop fails, and the fields lie empty and barren; even though the flocks die in the fields, and the cattle barns are empty, yet I will rejoice in the Lord! I will be joyful in the God of my salvation. The Sovereign Lord is my strength! He will make me as surefooted as a deer, able to tread upon the heights" (Habakkuk 3:17–19).

Though you may feel otherwise, there will always be something for you to do that will contribute toward your breakthrough and your realization of the abundant life God has promised you. And remember, far more rests upon God's shoulders than on yours. Above all, He asks you to entrust yourself to Him.

Something supernatural happens when we commit ourselves into the Father's care and then take only the steps that He tells us to. We don't shrink back in fear and intimidation; we don't get bitter or full of self-pity; instead, we bravely take initiative with a humble, hopeful heart. God loves you and He knows your situation inside and out. He wants to lighten the load and renew your heart amidst this heavy season of marriage if you'll let Him. Please let Him.

Often during these one-sided seasons, the Enemy of your soul will threaten you with fears and anxieties about your future. One of his age-old tricks is to use a painful past to create a fearful future. No doubt your husband has made some mistakes in the past. He may be making mistakes now. It is especially easy to worry if you think your husband holds your future in the palm of his hands.

How vulnerable it is to think that if your husband drops the ball, he drops you! And yet God's Word says that if you belong to *Him*, your future rests secure. There is forgiveness in Christ. There is redemption and renewal in Christ. God can even redeem our mistakes. No matter how your husband may fail, or how the Enemy tries to threaten or frighten you, know that Satan's doom is sure, and so is your deliverance.

We don't have to control everything; we can't. But God can. And because He is in control, we don't have to worry. Everyone who trusts in the Lord will eventually find themselves in divinely arranged circumstances that are prearranged to prove and prepare them for God's blessings and breakthroughs.

□

In 1 Samuel we read about King Saul, who was overcome with jealousy and insecurity because of the young man David, who obviously had the favor of the Lord upon his life. Even though David treated King Saul with honor and respect, Saul threw spears, grew in hatred, and conspired to kill David. David ran for his life and often hid in caves. You can probably relate to David as you may also be experiencing times of injustice and unfair treatment. When the weight shifts in marriage, almost always a sense of injustice follows.

This should go without saying, but if you are in any kind of physical danger—as David was—please run for help, and God will use people to give you the practical help you need.

If you are enduring a season in marriage where your love and service are returned with selfishness, suspicion, distraction, or even apathy, entrust yourself to the Lord. He will come through for you. It was during David's desperate times that he penned some of the most beautiful, prayerful expressions ever written. As you lean in to your protective heavenly Father and allow Him to pour His comfort and healing balm into your soul, something beautiful will come from you too (be sure to write down what He gives you; it will be a treasure for years to come).

Anytime we choose to refuse worry and walk forward in faith, God will be there to meet us. Try if you can to picture Jesus on the path ahead of you, clearing the rocks and the thickets, making a way for you. Imagine Him beside you, encouraging you onward, offering to carry your bag for a while, or *you*, for that matter. Listen to Him whisper words of faithfulness and courage as you put one foot in front of the other. He is totally engaged on this journey with you.

The Lord directs the steps of the godly. He delights in every detail of their lives. Though they stumble, they will never fall, for the Lord holds them by the hand. Once I was young, and now I am old. Yet I have never seen the godly abandoned or their children begging for bread. (Psalm 37:23–25)

⸺⸻⸺

When we refuse peace and embrace worry, we end up weighing ourselves down with far more than God Himself would ever ask us to carry.

When our circumstances threaten to bury us, it means we are carrying more than our share either literally or emotionally (or both). When I encounter such times, I now whisper a prayer, "Dear Lord, what part of this are You supposed to be carrying? Please help me to release it to You. You promised that Your yoke is easy and Your burden is light; help me to walk in Your way."

While it is true that life can be painfully heavy and trying, weighing us down, it is even truer that God is wonderfully strong and loving. Furthermore, as we discard the perception that the world is on our shoulders and confess that we are nothing without Christ, but can do all things through Him, we will come to know and believe that far more is up to Him than up to us. We were made to worship Him, not to worry about things that are no match for His power.

How big is the container that holds your worry? Is it bigger than your capacity for God? How often does worry spill over into other areas of your life? Acknowledge the things you worry about; confess them to your heavenly Father, and find a verse that nourishes your soul during this season. Keep that verse closer to your heart than your tendency to worry. You'll notice that as the

Scripture comes to life, worry is less apt to overtake your life.

Know that the Enemy of your soul is alive and active. He seeks to weigh you down with a load of worry that will take you off course and steal your joy. Every day, check your bags; and if your worry has reappeared, bring it before the Lord, and leave it with Him. Determine to make this journey without the added weight of worry. Have peace instead. You will be glad you did.

"Guide me in your truth and teach me, for you are God my Savior, and my hope is in you all day long" (Psalm 25:5 NIV).

LENDING A HAND

Watch Your Step—Are you worried that this season will be unbearable? That your marriage will never improve? That you can't pay the bills? These concerns are real, but even so, be careful not to think longer about your circumstances than you do about God and His great love for you. Though your marriage isn't all you want it to be, God is all you could ever need and more. In fact, especially in this season, may your thoughts gravitate toward how deeply you are loved by God. This will nourish your soul and protect you from worry.

Stay on the Right Path—Remember to think on what is admirable and worthy of praise. Take every worrying thought captive and make it bow to the living God! Dwell on the faithfulness of God. Remember to think about all the ways God has come through for you in the past. Remember to replace worry with thankfulness every single day.

Run From—Run from vain imaginations and "what-ifs." Take care of what you need to, and release the rest. Run from trying to control everything yourself. Run from trying to fix or change your husband. Ruth Graham once said, "It's my job to love Billy. It's God's job to make him good."

Destination Ahead—Run toward your heavenly Father every minute of the day. Every chance you get, turn your thoughts toward Jesus and the fact that He bore every burden on the cross. Seek peace and pursue it. Turn your back on worry, and turn your eyes toward faith.

Watch the Fine Line—Don't let your mind become obsessed with worry. Refuse to allow your thoughts to control you. But don't confuse "not thinking" about these things with never facing what you are worrying about. Put ample time into what you can do about the things weighing heavy on you, but then release the outcome to the Lord.

God's Promise for You Today—"When I said, 'My foot is slipping,' your love, O LORD, supported me. When anxiety was great within me, your consolation brought joy to my soul" (Psalm 94:18–19 NIV).

Precious Lord,

You are all that I need. Forgive me for wasting countless moments worrying when I could instead be praying and walking on in faith. You have called me to a higher way. Help me to shift my hopes, dreams, and fears onto Your almighty shoulders. Help me, too, to carry only what You provide each day. I long to live a life of such trust and obedience that there will be no doubt to the world that You are living in me. I bow my knee before You today and give You the things that are weighing heavy upon me. In Jesus' name, I refuse to allow worry to overtake my life. Fill me instead with peace so that it

□

spills over and brings clarity to every area of my life! Now, Lord, may I ask You, what's on Your heart for me today? How can I obey You in this place? Lead me on. Amen.

TO THINK ABOUT...

1. Read Philippians 4:6

a. Write down everything you are worrying about right now.

b. Sometimes putting our worry behind us is simply a matter of turning our back on it and deciding to trust God instead. For every item you listed, write out a faith-filled prayer stating God's faithfulness (e.g., *"I thank You, Lord, that You are my provider and You guard all that is mine. You will supply all my needs."*).

c. Every time you feel a twinge of worry creep up, determine to stop in your tracks and tell God what you need. Think about the common places and times when you worry. Write down a plan that works for you, one that helps you obey God and refuse worry.

d. Write down everything for which you are thankful.

2. Read Philippians 4:7

If you determine to turn your back on worry and trust the Lord instead, and if you keep your prayer life alive and embrace a grateful heart, what promise is yours for the taking?

☐

Write out several faith statements that connect what you are promised in this verse to what you've been worrying about (e.g., "I will have_____ about my future because I choose to trust the Lord.").

3. Read Psalm 139:23–24

a. Take a minute and write this passage out in a personalized prayer. Look at the study questions from chapter 1 if you need a reminder on how to get started.

b. Time for listening prayer! Write a personalized love letter to yourself from your heavenly Father. I'll give you a little help, *"My precious daughter, if you could see things from My perspective, you wouldn't have a worry in the world. I want you to remember . . . "*

4. Is there a recurring issue that keeps you in the cycle of worry? Write it down. Determine to put in three hours this week to work toward solving this issue. Is it finances? Put three hours into organizing your bills, calling a financial counselor, or asking for the help you need. Is it your husband's walk of faith? Take three hours this week to pray specifically for him so that you can entrust him once again to God. If your situation doesn't allow for your intervention, take that time to nourish your soul and your body. Take a hot bath, spend some extra time in prayer, and read a good book. Make the time to take on those things that wear you out with worry! Write down your plan.

Three

FEAR

*Do not fear anything except the Lord Almighty. He alone is
the Holy One. If you fear him, you need fear nothing else.*

□ Isaiah 8:13 NLT

I ONCE went on a trip that took me well away from where I was most comfortable. I had a packing list I didn't understand, I was going into a culture I knew little about, and I was leaving behind many of the things that made my world feel unruffled and secure.

What could *I* possibly say to a group of Belizean women, some who lived in poverty and some who had either been beaten or abandoned by their husbands—or both?

The plane landed and our team was met by a sweet, short Belizean man wearing a battered red baseball cap. He loaded our bags on his old bus and we were on our way. I clutched the seat in front of me as he drove, whistling, and whipped down a road that was too narrow for two lanes of traffic *and* mothers walking along, carrying their babies. But there we were, all on the same road, and nobody else seemed to feel the need to be stressed but me.

□

Once we got closer to the mission base, my friend Ann pointed up to a steep foothill and said, "We're staying in that building, on top of that hill." I swallowed hard, clutched the seat with a little more grit, and wondered how and if this old bus would get up that mountain.

When we got to the base of the hill, the team leaders said, "Okay, everyone! Pray this bus makes it up the hill!" The driver revved the engine. The bus rocked back and forth, trying to garner the strength for the steep climb. All at once the driver punched it down and the bus chugged up the hill, grabbing bits of gravel every few feet.

Suddenly the driver took a turn to the left, and the bus started to tilt. I looked out my window down an embankment and wondered how many dead bodies were scattered around down there. Our team leaders yelled out, "Everyone to the right side of the bus!"

We all jumped to the right side of the bus to counterbalance the weight. The driver took another turn, we again started to tilt, and we jumped to the left side of the bus.

Once we conquered the mountain and I got my legs to quit shaking, we were taken to our rooms. Mine was the only room with a scorpion on the floor. Hmm.

At dinnertime we met the driver's wife and their little children—what a lovely family this was! During dinner a young man came in the side door and spoke briefly with the couple. He had a street-smart way about him that was unsettling to me. When he left, I asked about him. The bus driver replied, "He was once a serial killer. He killed three people by putting a gun in their mouths. He was a juvenile when he did this and went to jail for a few years. When he got out, he came to me for a job but I told him, 'You're in no shape to work for me; come *live* with me instead. I'll teach you about Jesus.'"

Almost every major fear that dwelled deep within me was confronted on this trip. For example, when I was young, a traumatizing experience with a group of teenaged boys left me more fearful than I should have been of young men I didn't know. Now here I was in the same room with a killer. Another time, I was in a car accident and my head smashed into the windshield. I feared vehicles I couldn't control, and here I was going uphill in a rickety bus. And there was that time my sister and I got lost in a terrible part of town and had to hide in our car while a group of gang members lurked about not too far from us. It took me a long time to develop the desire to travel after that. Now here I was traveling in a different country, meeting people with scary backgrounds, riding in a vehicle that seemed to be on its last legs.

Because I was carrying fears from the past, my present circumstances seemed overwhelmingly frightening. Yet if you asked the other team leaders about their experience with our trip from the airport to the mission base, they would smile and say, "It was so good to be back in Belize again. We had a great first day!"

What was true about my scary circumstances is that our sweet little bus driver may have been short in stature, but he was a giant of a man. He is the mayor of a local city. He's led several high-ranking officials to Christ. And he was perfectly capable of driving that bus. He has a vision for Belize, he's a mover and a shaker, he is dialed into that community, and he is making a difference there. We were safe in his care. Even the streetwise young man, a onetime killer, had given his life to Christ and works hard around the mission base. I was completely inspired by these radical, wonderful people.

Fear will ruin our journey. Fear will skew our perspective. Fear keeps us from taking in all of what God wants to show us. Fear will affect everything we do.

Open your bag, look inside for a moment: Are you packing fear? Do you find current records of old circumstances? Do you remember by heart what happened and how it made you feel? Are there situations that trigger your fears and make you queasy? Is it poverty that you fear, or maybe abandonment? Do you realize how heavy this makes your journey?

Determine today to leave fear behind. How to do this, you ask? You might need a friend, a pastor, or a godly counselor to pray you through this process. Ask God to show you what lie you picked up when life let you down. Perhaps repeated financial struggles have left you with a fear of continual lack. And yet God's Word says, "And my God will supply all your needs according to His riches in glory in Christ Jesus" (Philippians 4:19 HCSB). Maybe your father abandoned you, or your husband repeatedly threatens to leave. This is a big fear to overcome, but there is provision for you. God's Word promises, "Be strong and courageous. Do not be afraid or terrified . . . for the LORD your God goes with you; he will never leave you nor forsake you" (Deuteronomy 31:6 NIV).

What wrong beliefs have you carried because your fears have deceived you? Ask Jesus to help you search the Scriptures for a corresponding promise that will set you free. Begin to rid yourself of fear today. At least, start today and determine not to be bullied, manipulated, or deceived by your fears.

SPIRITUAL LIFT:

"Whatever foes may be before the Christian, they are all overcome. There are lions but their teeth are broken; there are serpents, but their fangs are extracted; there are rivers but they are bridged or fordable; there are flames, but we wear that matchless garment which renders us invulnerable to fire."

Charles Spurgeon[1]

Years ago my husband was very sick. He recovered from cancer surgery only to get sicker from the radiation treatments. One night his spinal cord swelled from the treatments, and his jaw locked up from the anti-nausea medication. Since it was too painful for him to lie down, and he was too exhausted to be up, he stayed in bed by being on all fours. Holding his jaw and resting on his elbows, he rocked back and forth, shifting his weight from his elbows to his knees, desperately praying, "Oh God, Oh God, Oh Jesus."

I tried to pray for him, but his skin hurt too much for me to touch him. I grabbed a fistful of his pillow, buried my face in it, and prayed for his relief. I was unsettled to my core watching my big, strong husband being reduced to such a fragile state of health.

I had a new thing to fear.

For instance, because of what God had already allowed to happen in our lives, I feared He would allow even worse things to happen to us. I feared He wouldn't come through for us. I looked to people to meet needs that were God's to fill. When I had "faith," it was because people knew my need and not so much because God did. Joyce Meyer says, "Too often we go to the phone instead of the Throne." Well, I went to the phone *and* the Throne, but I always seemed to trust that people would come through for me long before God ever would.

Somehow in a night's time, I managed to pull the weight of the world on top of my shoulders. The mixture of trivial and important questions that ran through my mind surprised me.

How will I work the furnace when he's gone? *He later told me that the furnace runs itself.* Will we have to move? *We have insurance.* How will our sons turn out without a father? *They have a heavenly Father.* Will I become a wrinkled, timid widow? *That depends on me, I guess.*

I made sure Kevin took his vitamins. I made sure he ate well. I even regularly patted him down looking for lumps and bumps that might threaten his health. Eventually I realized that his life was in God's hands, not mine.

Fear makes us do crazy things. My friend joked the other day, "Let's say I have a fear of spiders. Which is worse, seeing the spider or breaking my leg trying to get away from one?"

Fear makes us see things that are not there. Unless we resolve our fears, they will continually deceive us. For many of us, our fears were born out of painful experiences that have stuck with us. We fear rejection, pain, disappointing others, and losing the things that we love. When we don't resolve the inconsistent messages our experiences leave us with, we begin to trust and cling to our fears more than we trust and cling to God.

A few years ago, at the height of the economic downturn, my husband was laid off from a high-paying software job. At the time, I was enjoying my role as an at-home mom after many years of working outside the home. So when my husband asked if he could use the layoff as an opportunity to pursue his long-time dream of starting his own company, my response was anything but supportive.

I was afraid. We had a mortgage, car payments, bills, and all the other expenses that a growing family accumulates. My sincere desire to support and comfort him grappled with my honest concern about keeping my family secure and provided for. But after much discussion, we decided to try out his idea for three months to see if it could work.

Three months stretched into more than a year. During that time, I pleaded for him to go out and find a job. I bargained and threatened, but nothing I did changed anything. I felt that the longer and more strongly I opposed my husband's effort to turn his dreams into a viable and profitable company, the more stubborn he became.

I felt frustrated and angry most of the time, and I wondered why God wasn't doing anything about it. What I thought were faithful prayers sounded like this: "Please help me get everything back to normal. And could You do it right away?" But as things moved further away from our old routine, I grew more afraid and more resentful every day.

Even among my closest friends, I sealed my fears inside. My

attitude was, "We're all fine; now let's change the subject." It was difficult for me to admit I needed their support. Always the one known as the giver, I was ashamed now to confess that things weren't going so well, and after awhile I simply stopped showing up at outings with my friends.

Then one day, after months of trying to change things to the way I wanted them, I found Psalm 63:8, and it spoke directly to my heart: "My soul clings to you; your right hand upholds me."

I realized that I'd been holding on to God with one hand while trying to fix things and do things my way with the other. But this verse gave me the courage to let go of my ways and allow myself to cling to God completely.

When I sincerely and fully surrendered this situation to God, I was no longer afraid. I knew He was in charge of things now. Soon I experienced more peace, and joy returned to my heart; and I was able to confess my fears—the root of my anger—to my husband, and our communication improved from there. He understood my feelings, and having given up control, I could sincerely consider and support his desires.

This change of heart allowed me to champion my husband (who had also suffered from my anger and fear) and consider positive options that strengthened our marriage, our family, and my faith through that difficult time. For example, I took a part-time job, which brought in steady income while my husband's business was still building, and it allowed me to focus on a steady, daily routine.

My husband and I became stronger together; he plunged into his work, our children adjusted to the switch in roles, and they took on more chores around the house.

> Most important, I learned to trust God more deeply every
> day as I walk in His will and rest in His love.
>
> —Marilyn from California

We all have a "pain pendulum" that compels us to react when we are first hurt in some way. Then, later on in life when situations arise that are remotely reminiscent to our initial memory, we tend to overreact and overcompensate, and our beliefs are once again confirmed that people and circumstances (and sometimes God) cannot be trusted.

Until we are willing to dig beneath the surface and reconcile our wrong beliefs and fears with the wonderful truths of God, we will be held captive by our past experiences. Unless we deal with our fears, the beliefs about our painful past experiences will continue to hurt us because they will continually translate into current wrong beliefs.

Though I am pretty frugal, I at times purchased things in haste rather than humbly waiting and trusting God with the desires of my heart. I ate more food than I needed when I felt lonely or frustrated or mad. I spent too much time with friends when my emptiness was really compelling me to spend more time with Him. I even put up a defensive wall with my husband when it *appeared* he might let me down again.

One day I marched to the store and bought myself something I couldn't afford and yet felt I needed; or maybe *deserved* is a better word. I heard the Lord speak to me: *Why do you do that, Susie? Is it because you don't believe that I am good and that I love you and have promised to take care of you?*

I realized right then and there how many of my actions were motivated by a certain mistrust of God. Though I had an active devotional life, deep in my heart I didn't believe in God's love and provision. Every time I let go of the truth that God profoundly loves me and has pledged Himself to me, I also let go of every good reason for making healthy, faith-filled choices.

Fears are real and the Enemy will use them to manipulate us all day long (if he can get away with it). It isn't until we face our fears and acknowledge how they affect us that we realize that God is much bigger than all our past memories or potential heartaches.

Try this: Write your fears on a piece of paper. Lift up your fears and declare, "My fears are paper thin! They have no power over me anymore! God is my constant supply, my help in time of need, and my divine protection! God is alive and active and I will overcome these fears with faith!" Then have a bonfire and watch your fears turn to ashes.

What powerful lives await us when we put our fears in the past where they belong and we start really believing in God's love and provision! Let's look at the verse at the beginning of this chapter again:

"Do not fear *anything* except the Lord Almighty. He alone is the Holy One. If you fear him, you need fear *nothing else*" (Isaiah 8:13 NLT).

While this passage gives us an exception, it does not say, "Do not fear anything except rejection" or "Do not fear anything except the future." We are not to fear ANYTHING with the exception of the Lord. What does it mean to fear the Lord? To me, fearing the Lord means I will do what He says, because I know He will do what He says.

To walk in the fear of the Lord is to know that while God is love, He means what He says about sin, bad attitudes, and unforgiveness. To walk in the fear of the Lord means to keep our hearts pure and our minds set on obeying Him. To give the Lord the respect and reverence He is due is to face the things that scare us and then look past them to the One who can do something about our fears.

HIS WORD—OUR SWORD

The Word of God is our Sword—our offensive weapon—given to us to cut through the lies of the Enemy (read Ephesians 6:10–18). The more we spend time reading, memorizing, and nourishing our souls in the Word of God, the better we become at wielding the Sword. Pack your Sword, not your fears.

I meet far too many women (in fact, I was one myself), who leave their Swords in their closets. They live tormented by their fears, they make choices based on their fears, they expect things from their husbands that God already promised to give them, and they forget all about the weapon provided them for such a time as this.

Instead of fighting for their marriage, they worry about it. Instead of praying for a breakthrough, they pore over their own list of woes. Instead of believing a life of promise is possible, they camp in the wilderness of despair. God is just as big in us as He was in David when he fought Goliath!

Regarding my own life, I was always amazed that God would not rescue me from some of the scariest battles I encountered. Let me rephrase that. He rescued me from pain, depression, rejection, and desperate circumstances that threatened to crush me. But when it came to the lies that accompanied those experiences, I felt like the son who was having a scuffle in the yard with the neighbor boy while the father watched from the kitchen window, fully aware of the fight, but wanting his child to learn how to defend himself.

It wasn't until I became worn out from being bullied by my fears that I finally decided to learn how to use the weapon God gave me. I began to memorize Scripture. I pondered certain passages for a long time until they sank deep into my soul. I quoted passages out loud on the good days, and twice as often on the bad days. (Buy index cards that are spiral-bound. You can stand them up, read Scripture out loud, and then flip to the next one. This discipline is a *must* for the journey.)

When I heard myself speak out the living, breathing Word of God, my faith grew, and with it my understanding of my authority in Christ. I came to understand that the Devil was a trespasser and would continue to be unless I drew my Sword, lifted my shield of faith, and refused to allow his lies and his threats to weaken me.

Know your rights as a child of God. Use the spoken Word of God; it is your greatest weapon. When you apply yourself to this task, something supernatural will happen before your eyes.

You will go from being battered by your fears to being brave in the face of them; you will go from feeling victimized by your circumstances to being the victor Christ called you to be; and most important, you will turn your back on the lies of the Enemy, and come to understand and *experience* who you are and what you possess in Christ.

"Let the praises of God be in their mouths, and a sharp sword in their hands" (Psalm 149:6).

A quick reminder: This is a discipline that takes practice. You may stumble and fall a few times, and you may not see instant results. But when you *consistently* believe what the Bible says, and you take God at His Word, you will eventually see your giants go down, your fears crumble, and your faith in the power of God increase.

☐

HIS HEART—OUR HOME

Some think that to fear the Lord means to cower before Him in hopes that He won't accidentally step on us and squash us like a bug. Yet while God is greater than any of us can comprehend and far more powerful than the greatest mind can know, He is also our Savior and our friend. He is intimately acquainted with all our ways and longs for us to trust Him. There is no one greater than God. He looks at the oceans and they stir up. He glances at the mountains and they tremble. The trees clap their hands in amazement of who He is (see Isaiah 55:12). But still, God wants us near.

Our call to walk in the awe and reverence of the Lord is a call to understand that He is both an awesome and an intimate God. He wants us so comfortable with His love that we come boldly into His presence at a moment's notice. He wants us calling on Him every time we think of it. He wants us to trust Him, and He longs to show us just how faithful He is.

In order for us not to fear anything except the Lord, we must be at home in the presence of God; we must know that He is on this journey with us even when we can't feel Him. We must trust in His unfailing love.

Surrender your husband to the Lord. Surrender your children. Surrender your imperfections and frustrations. Surrender the demand that everything must go your way. Surrender your hopes and dreams. And most important, surrender your fears. Lay them at His feet, and pick up your Sword. (You may have to do this again and again. But don't give up.)

What are you afraid of right now? Write down your fears in a notebook or journal. Find corresponding Scriptures and write them next to or under these fears. Write the Scriptures in prayer form and pray these prayers daily.

Rid yourself of them, every day if that's what your day requires. "Do not be afraid, for I am with you" (Isaiah 43:5). "Fear-of-God is a school in skilled living—first you learn humility, then you experience glory" (Proverbs 15:33 THE MESSAGE).

You are an overcomer! Take a deep breath in and gently exhale. With every breath you take, acknowledge your breath as a gift from a God who wants you around because He has a plan for your life.

LENDING A HAND

Watch Your Step—Be careful about what comes out of your mouth. Are you giving voice to your fears more often than wielding your Sword? The fears that threaten to crush you will stand back when your words become consistent with God's Word. Stand on the promises of God, and then you'll be less apt to trip over the lies of the Enemy. "From the fruit of his lips a man is filled with good things as surely as the work of his hands rewards him" (Proverbs 12:14 NIV).

Stay on the Right Path—Remember who God is and who you are to Him. He is to be treated with reverence and awe. He is also to be embraced and loved. You are everything to Him. Trust Him. Remember that as big as the fears about your circumstances feel to you, God is bigger still.

Run From—Run from the temptation to grab quick solutions that cover up your fears. Determine not to make fear-based choices. When you deal with the depth of your fear, you'll dance with joy when you've been set free!

Destination Ahead—Run toward the Word, godly friends, and good books. Fill your heart and mind with things that challenge, inspire, and remind you of who you are to Jesus. *"Perfect love casts out fear"* (1 John 4:18 NASB). Familiarize yourself with God's great love for you; remind yourself every day that you are the object of God's love (and so is your husband), and your fears will fall by the wayside.

Watch the Fine Line—While it is important not to give too much time voicing your fears, it is also important that you not suppress them. Be honest when you are struggling. Call a godly friend and ask her to pray for you. There is a big difference between bashing your husband without any fear of the Lord, and sincerely seeking counsel and encouragement to stay on the right track. Guard and nourish your heart so you can fight the good fight.

God's Promise for You Today—"Do not be afraid . . . *I have called you by name; you are mine.* When you go through deep waters, I will be with you. When you go through rivers of difficulty, you will not drown. When you walk through the fire of oppression, you will not be burned up; the flames will not consume you" (Isaiah 43:1–2).

Precious Father,

I lift up my painful memories of yesterday and my fears for tomorrow, and I ask You to come. Come with Your truth and set me free. Help me to know what it means to live every day in awe of You. More and more may I come to know the power and strength of Your love. Lead me to Scriptures that match my circumstances; help me get better at using my Sword. Remind me with every sunrise that I have nothing to fear because You are with me. I am Yours and You are mine. I will place my fears before You and pick up faith instead. I will trust You with my heart today. Amen.

TO THINK ABOUT...

1. Read Psalm 91

a. Read this chapter again, but this time make it personal and read it out loud (e.g., "I will not be afraid of the terrors of the night, nor fear the dangers of the day . . . ").

b. Describe what it means to live in His shelter.

c. When we *live* in His shelter, what do we find? Why do you suppose this is a by-product of walking closely with the Lord? Explain.

2. Read verses 5–6 again

a. Rewrite these verses in a descriptive way that matches your circumstances. For instance, what are some of the fears that plague you at night? Insert them into your written passage. When you're done, you should have a paragraph-long, paraphrased scriptural declaration that addresses the things in *your* life.

3. Read verses 9–13 again

a. Write this passage in a personalized prayer.

b. Time again for listening prayer, but this time I want you to use verses 14–16 as a guideline. Begin your listening prayer like this, "My precious one, I have promised to rescue you, because you love Me. I will protect you because . . . "

4. Memorize Isaiah 41:10 and say it out loud whenever you need to.

Four

SELF-PITY

*An undisciplined, self-willed life is puny;
an obedient, God-willed life is spacious.*

Proverbs 15:32 THE MESSAGE

CAN I ASK you to consider unpacking one more item? Are you traveling with an oversized magnifying glass? Do you have the ability or tendency to over analyze your situation until it becomes larger than life? Don't feel bad; we all do. But how often do you pull that thing out and make an all-too-close account of what *bugs* you about your life and your husband?

I remember when my boys were young. One of their favorite things to do in the summer was to take a magnifying glass, get as low to the ground as they could, and look for bugs. Little critters became life-sized, and for those few moments, my boys were inhabitants in the land of the creepy crawlies. Of course, looking at the bugs wasn't all they were after. I am sorry to say they quickly figured out that if you angle the glass just right, you catch the sun; when the sun is magnified and aimed at the bugs, you get fried critters in a matter of seconds.

Eventually my boys joined the rest of us in the land of the giants, and it was enough for them to just put the bugs under their feet.

Imagine if my boys were looking downward for bugs while walking on a cliff's edge with the magnifying glass pressed up against their faces. You can imagine what I, as a mother, would do.

When our marriage falls out of balance and life begins to feel heavy, it is good to take inventory of our lives and our commitments. It's good to assess how these things are affecting our inner lives. It's important to make adjustments when seasons change; because balance is a fluid, organic thing, and it's something to which we must always pay attention. However, we must not spend too much time looking through the magnifying glass at all that is wrong in our lives.

If, while walking through painful and disappointing seasons in our marriage, we dwell on, become obsessed with, and can think only about our problems, we wander dangerously close to the edge of the cliff, which overlooks the canyon of defeat. When our focus gets so narrow that we only see ourselves, we diminish our strength and perspective. Our world shrinks and our problems are magnified. Our impact in this world is reduced, and our burden increased. Our ability to see the bigger picture is replaced with a disproportionate, pinhole view of life. Nothing good can come from a self-absorbed mind-set.

When we put our faces to the ground and repeatedly count and analyze all of the bugs in our lives, we run the risk of wandering off the path of godly perspective, which is the very road that will lead us out of the wilderness.

□

Over and over again I have heard from women who don't know how to console or counsel their dear friend or sister who is drowning in self-pity and obsessed with the "hunt." Yes, their situations are difficult and unfair, but to watch their loved ones put their sad faces in the dirt and dissect every bitter-critter in their lives is heartbreaking. The one on the "hunt" has lost perspective, is sure that no one has it harder than she does, and has stopped listening to anyone else's story. Hers has become a small world after all.

We all have our woe-filled days, but it is essential that we find our way back to the path of humility, perspective, and gratitude once again.

Below is a portion of an e-mail I received from a very godly woman who has been walking through a long and very trying season in her marriage:

> *Self-pity!* I vacillate between trusting God and feeling lots of self-pity! I feel it when I look at those around me, and watch my years slipping away. I'm not getting any younger and I don't get to do the fun things I always dreamed about. Mostly when I hear about something fun someone else has done, I feel self-pity. Just this morning on my way to work, I was thinking about all the things I have to do . . . alone. I attend events, buy groceries, and so on . . . alone.
>
> The only thing worse than being alone is being alone with someone sitting right beside you. My husband is in such a deep depression that he finds it very difficult to leave the house, or leave the couch, for that matter. I try and find the fine line

between encouraging him to get out and do things and just leaving him alone. It's a very difficult line; pushing too hard can do more harm; not pushing him a little leaves me feeling guilty for not trying to help him pull out of the depression. This leaves me in the position to do many things alone.

The other day I was at the grocery store and a man started pushing my cart by accident. His wife looked at him . . . and he looked at her . . . then at me again. I teased them by saying I don't need one of those . . . I already have one waiting for me at home (a man, that is). We all laughed, but then every time I passed them in the aisles, I felt a little dumb and very alone. Many people shop alone, no big deal; it's just that we used to shop together, so I really feel the void.

I have a few things coming up that most women would attend with their husbands. I will be going alone. One is a boat trip with my family. I'm sure he won't be up to going. I cried to God just this morning; I didn't get married to be alone! Then I felt bad, of course. When I'm not trusting God with my future and I look at what others have, then I feel self-pity.

When I get back in the Word, or read devotionals, I feel better. Today is just a little harder than normal. Maybe it's when we are weak or tired or struggling with PMS that we allow self-pity to grow.

And yet, when I think about my son, my self-pity fades into the background. I am so grateful to God for him. Whenever I feel defeated in marriage, I just have to look at my son and I feel victorious again. I think it's because of his heart. I know how much he loves God. Who could want anything more? I pity others because they don't have him!

Really, God has been taking very good care of me—

making up for many of the things I don't have with my husband.
God is always doing little things that only I would notice. You
just have to notice the small things. They are everywhere.

I have this dear friend who has helped me more than
anything else to get through this difficult time. Every time I start
to lose hope, there she is to pick me up off the floor, to lean on
when I'm starting to lose hope, or when I need a dose of courage.
She reminds me to take care of myself and do nice things for
myself. I really never would have lasted this long without my
friend. I'm like one of those old windup toys; every time there's
just a few clicks left, I call her up and she winds me up again.

Regarding my marriage, I absolutely do not accept that this
is a permanent situation. I know in my deepest places that God
will restore my husband to health—and our marriage as well. I
just don't know when. I so strongly believe in God's timing; I
don't want him back a minute sooner than God is ready to give
him back. (Okay, sometimes I do, but then I come around.) I
completely trust that God wants the absolute best for my
husband. That means for now I need to do my best to keep from
falling into the dark hole with him. I try and find a few things
that I can do with him so we aren't complete strangers. Then
other times I just have to get mad at him and my situation and
go walk through a mall or go hang out in a coffee shop with a
good book by myself.

During this difficult time, God has surprised me with a
new job. Many blessings have gone along with it, unexpected
things that someone else may never have noticed. Little gifts for
my heart alone, like cable TV. We had to give it up because of
my husband's unemployment. In the room right next to me at
work, there is a huge plasma TV, and at least once a week it's

turned on—and to HGTV, my favorite channel—right there for me to watch! It's like a little secret between God and me. His whisper spoke loudly to me, "I know how much you miss this show, and I'm sorry for all you've had to give up. Hope this helps." You could have knocked me over with a feather!

I'm constantly surprised by little gifts just like this. It's not so much the gift, but the fact that He cares that I'm hurting and knows what I'm giving up. He notices every little detail! I feel so important to God. I love my husband so much. I am not willing to give him up. I'm going to stick by his side as long as it takes. I know that's what God wants. No, it isn't easy; it's very, very hard, but in the end I expect to have a husband who loves and understands the Lord the way I do. He will be the spiritual leader of my family, just the way God wants it.

That will be more than worth the wait.

—Lynn from Minneapolis

Did you notice in her e-mail how she went from despair to perspective, from grieving to remembering? She had her woeful moments, and understandably so; but then she walked herself back to a place of gratitude and perspective. And she is right about noticing the small blessings. Sometimes these bread crumbs are the very things God uses to help us find our way through the wilderness.

Even the most mature Christian is a candidate for self-pity. But I guess you don't need to read her story to know how easy it is to feel sorry for yourself.

Who doesn't struggle with self-pity *once in a while*? Sometimes a good bout of self-pity sounds as enticing as a tasty bowl of ice cream. Just a little won't hurt, right? But we never have just a little. We pull out three flavors and a giant spoon. We fill up our medium-sized mixing bowl and take a glance around the room in case anyone is watching. We drizzle on the chocolate and the caramel and maybe even a crumbled cookie.

We never intend to eat the whole thing, but we almost always have more than we should. Ice cream tastes great, but indulging regularly will weigh us down and diminish our health. This is where the application ends, though. A *little* ice cream every now and then can actually be a positive thing, but a little self-pity never will.

John W. Gardner wrote, "Self-pity is easily the most destructive of the non-pharmaceutical narcotics; it is addictive, gives momentary pleasure and separates the victim from reality." And Andre Maurois wrote, "Self-pity comes so naturally to all of us. The most solid happiness can be shaken by the compassion of a fool."[1]

The most solid happiness can be shaken by the compassion of a fool. During times of self-pity, we don't need a party, and we especially don't need the compassion of a fool. In other words, we may have a genuine gripe; we may have good reason for unhappiness; and yet *always* in the midst of such times, when we look for them, we can find profound reasons for praise.

The fool not only forgets to remind you of such things; she will pity you as if your situation is hopeless, which it isn't. She will long for your approval more than your victory and will sing your pity song as long as you will listen. We don't need favors like these. What we need is the strength to pray and the courage to repent.

There will be days when we have every legitimate reason to

fall into a slump of self-pity—but self-pity is not our friend; it is a cancerous tumor that threatens to steal the fresh life made available to us for the days in which we live. As Graham Cooke, one of my favorite authors, often says, "For every problem in life, there is a provision available from God; for every curse, there is a corresponding blessing appointed for me."

Rather than sympathize with the little pity parasite that seeks to grow within us, let's starve it, cut off its life source, and remove it from our midst! This is not to say that we're not allowed rainy days, down days, and days when we stay in our pajamas, watch chick flicks, and eat more than we should.

Everyone needs to step off the beaten path for a bit and acknowledge that life gets hard sometimes. But in our acknowledgment, we must never forget that *God is always good*, and He asks us to look up. Self-pity is always bad, and requires that we look down.

CAUTION: GRIEF AND SELF-PITY ARE NOT THE SAME

I have a good friend who said that during her alone time in marriage she was so determined not to entertain self-pity, that before she knew it, she was walking in complete denial. She said, "I denied all pain and was overly sensitive against any hint of self-pity within me; but I needed to face and acknowledge that *this was painful*. I needed to allow myself to feel the hurt, and this, I eventually learned, was *not* self-pity."

This is a very important point. The only way to *grow* through pain is going through it, not around it. Every year, we spend billions of dollars trying everything we can think of not to feel pain.

□

We shop, we eat, we read, we play, we overcommit, we medicate, and we look to the latest fad to be our detour. It's interesting how we embrace self-pity and run from pain.

And yet, like the scruffy stray pet we once fed but no longer want around, pain has a way of being patient, of not going anywhere, and of waiting for us when we get home. We have to feel it and deal with it in order to get it behind us.

If our season when it's all up to us is severe enough, we will most likely encounter a time of denial, of rearranging, or re-explaining what is happening in our life. Eventually though, we will stop pushing back and admit that our arms are tired and our hearts are broken. When we finally slow down and acknowledge that our path is a painful one, grief comes nipping at our heels.

   Grief stops running for a season.
   Grief is a part of life.
   Grief is a part of marriage.
   Grief teaches us.

Grief stops running for a season, sits in the muck, and sees life for the painful mess it is. Grief is a part of life. Grief is a part of marriage and grief can teach us many things. Grief teaches us to bring our disappointments to God. Grief teaches us that this world is not our home. Grief teaches us to hope in God more than we do people. But grief is still painful.

Real grief asks the questions: Is this real? Was *that* real? Is the dream I had for marriage gone? Will I ever feel good again? Will I even *like* the plan God has for me?

Grief acknowledges a loss of innocence and with it that once-wonderful sense of blissful naïveté. We admit that we don't want to know the things we've just learned.

Sometimes we grieve because our reality has been turned upside down. Other times we grieve the loss of "the princess dream." We had a pie in the sky idea of how we thought our married life should go. We were disillusioned to find that our Prince Charming had smelly socks and our Cinderella dreams were paper thin. We might be grieving an unrealistic illusion, but it is still painful.

God is gracious and wonderful and loving; He has made room for the process in which we deal with our pain. He has collected our tears in a bottle and will use every one of them to water the seeds of faith we sow. God is with us in our grief, but we must not confuse grief with self-pity.

- Self-pity is consumed with self and its entitlements.
- Self-pity is a temptation.
- Self-pity blinds us.
- Self-pity makes us ineffective.

Self-pity is consumed with its own comforts and constantly asks: Why is this happening to *me*? Why is life better for everyone else? Why doesn't God like me? Why won't anybody listen to me? Why do I have to live like this?

Grief cries out, "How will I ever get through this?" "What about my life is true?" "Where are You, God?" Self-pity shouts, "Nothing ever works out for me!"

Grief *feels* the loss inflicted by life—self-pity nurses the wound inflicted by self. Self-pity is grief's counterfeit.

To engage in self-pity is to make an idol out of our self-absorbed viewpoint. To engage in idolatry is to set something above the Lord Almighty. When we give more weight to *our* perspective of our spouse and our marriage than we do the promises of God, we make an idol out of *what we think we know*. Making this mistake offends the heart of God and will keep us from possessing the best of what God has for us.

On the other hand, when we see the pity parasite for what it is—something that will drain the life out of us if we allow it to—and we show it no mercy—we then by our obedience and courage position ourselves to receive a renewed and righteous perspective.

SPIRITUAL LIFT:

"Affliction comes to the believer not to make him sad, but sober; not to make him sorry, but wise. Even as the plow enriches the field so that the seed is multiplied a thousand fold, so affliction should magnify our joy and increase our spiritual harvest."

☐ *Henry Ward Beecher* 2

Don't let anyone rob you of your prize! Be assured; there is a reward in this for you! Be obedient in the painful times, and trust that God is up to something more grand and wonderful than you can imagine. If I could put my arms around you and hug you before writing this, I would, but consider it a gentle reminder from a friend: There is much more at stake here than your immediate comfort and happiness. And far more is at stake than the immediate issues in your marriage.

You are set apart by God Himself to affect the world around you. What seeds you sow will determine what you grow. Ask for the mind of Christ—ask for a perspective that matches His. Know that God has set you apart for Himself. He is your Husband, your Comforter, and your Friend; He *will* come through for you. Remember too that Jesus refused pity, but not comfort. Let Him comfort you. "When doubts filled my mind, your comfort gave me renewed hope and cheer" (Psalm 94:19).

Even in this place—where things are unfair, marriage is difficult, and others don't understand—God is faithful and He understands. You have an unusual opportunity here. In the midst of your very unique situation, you can find God, you can believe Him, and you can refuse self-pity.

Precious sister, I know you want to be much with God! And He wants to be big in you! Instead of clenched fists and low perspectives, bow low, open your hands, and look up. Don't hold your breath; don't *wait* for joy; it's yours today. Go after God until you realize the joy that's been made available to you. If you think you've gone too many days without being celebrated, think again . . . because every day the Savior celebrates and sings over you.

Get quiet, bow low, remove pity from your bag; remove the magnifying-glass mind-set that makes everything look bigger than it is. *Pack binoculars instead.* Get a far and wide view of where

God wants to take you. Look for His promise. Listen to His whisper, "*I love you, My daughter, and I'm in this with you. I am so sorry that your heart aches; I am acquainted with despair. But look up and listen; there is a host in the heavenlies cheering you onward! You are written on My hand and cherished in My heart. Listen, My child, I sing over you!*"

LENDING A HAND

Watch Your Step—Be careful about where you allow your thoughts to go. Every time you find yourself thinking thoughts of defeat, self-pity, overanalysis, get in the Word of God. Don't allow your perspective to be inconsistent with the promises of God.

Stay on the Right Path—Remember self-pity will diminish all that's wonderful about you! Do not be sympathetic to the little parasite; rid your life of this worm! The antidote for self-pity is worship. Put on a worshipful CD and listen to the lyrics; allow them to nourish your soul. Sing songs that declare God's goodness and faithfulness. Look up, not down.

Run From—Run from the compassion of a fool. Don't allow yourself to be a party to conversations with those who do not walk in the fear of the Lord. Memorize this verse, "May all who fear you find in me a cause for joy, for I have put my hope in your word" (Psalm 119:74).

Destination Ahead—Run toward every opportunity you find to be a blessing to others. Someone once said, "A person wrapped up in himself makes a very small package." On the flip side, a woman wrapped up in the love of God will be a vessel used by

Him no matter where life finds her. Throughout this difficult time, keep your eyes on the Lord and look for opportunities to minister to those who have less than you do.

Watch the Fine Line—Spend time with wise, godly people who will help you to know when you are overanalyzing or feeling sorry for yourself. Be teachable during this difficult time. But give yourself permission to admit when it is grief that you feel. Don't be afraid of gut-level honesty before the Lord. He will take you through the grief process. Understand, though, you will have days when grief can quickly turn to self-pity. When you stay close to Jesus, you'll more quickly discern this departure.

God's Promise for You Today—"You have turned my mourning into joyful dancing. You have taken away my clothes of mourning and clothed me with joy, that I might sing praises to you and not be silent. O Lord my God, I will give you thanks forever!" (Psalm 30:11–12).

Holy Father, Heavenly Bridegroom,

You are the One who loves me truly; inside and out; on my up days and my down days, You are there for me. Forgive me for the countless moments I have wasted feeling sorry for myself when I could have been praising You. You have blessed me beyond words, and when I look down, I lose sight of that. Draw me into a deeper relationship with You. You've promised to be my Husband and to fill every low place in my life. I will wait for You. I will look for You. Open my eyes to see what You are up to. Help me to trust You when I'd rather not. You are up to something much bigger than my eyes can see. Use this time in my life to build an eternal foundation of faith—one that will be passed down to future generations. I am Yours, Lord. Have Your way in me. Amen.

TO THINK ABOUT...

1. Read Psalm 29:10–11

a. The first two sentences speak of God's power and position. Write them down.

b. The second two sentences speak of God's provision for us. Write them down.

c. Most often when we venture into self-pity, it's because we have forgotten one of these aspects of who God is (His power, position, or provision). Looking at the verses above, which one of these perspectives is most apt to get away from you? Write it down and explain.

2. Read Romans 8:28–32, 37–38

a. Romans 8:28 says that God works ALL things together for those who are _____and _____. Do you believe you are? Loved and called, that is. In order to conquer the cancer of self-pity in our lives, we must not only remember who God is to us, we must remember *who we are to Him*. Write a declarative statement that addresses your issue in contrast with your call (e.g., *I will not feel sorry for myself for being alone too much, because I am treasured by God, and I have things to do in this life*).

b. Read verses 29 and 30 again. God knew you before time began; He had your destiny in mind before you were born. What was His ultimate goal for you (hint: to be conformed . . .)? Write it down. He not only predestined you, He _____, He _____, and He_____. Take a moment to personalize these four things. Write them in the left margin of your page, and then expound on what they mean for you specifically.

c. What obstacles and opposition are you up against right now? Write them down. Under that list, rewrite verses 30–31, and then step back and look at what you have written. God is on your side; you've got the advantage!

3. Read verses 37–38 again

a. Write this passage in a personalized prayer.

b. Time again for listening prayer. May your ears be open to the Lord's voice!

4. Journal today about something God is teaching you.

WEIGHTS THAT REFINE

DOESN'T IT feel great to lighten your load? I remember a time when I began cutting things from my all-too-busy schedule. I needed margins in my life, and God was making it clear which things needed to go. One at a time I pulled things out of my bag, tied up the loose ends, and then moved on without them. I was amazed at how much easier it was to walk and run and climb (and rest, for that matter) with a lighter load! So amazed was I that I was tempted to cut *everything* from my schedule—you know, clear off the counter, empty my plate, buy a new planner, and start fresh.

But there were some things God was still calling me to carry. As much as I loved the thought of skipping along and twirling my empty bag, I still had things to do, commitments to fulfill, and an adjusted yoke to carry.

Because of your divine importance in the whole scheme of things, you also have an adjusted yoke to carry. Your calling is a high one, and you must never lose sight of that truth. And when you're called, you're called to carry a yoke. Things that seem like unnecessary weights, or even obstacles, for that matter, are actually catalysts to your growth.

Not all weights that feel heavy should be dropped. Someone once said, "It's not the load that's heavy; it's the way we carry it."

In this next section we are going to talk about four refining weights that *can* be carried . . . just carried differently. As we venture along the path of marriage, we will deal with disappointment, loneliness, waiting, and imperfection.

Once again, we are going to look inside and take inventory. Will you take this next step toward growth and repack your bags? In other words, when you find these things on your journey, will you determine to hold them closer and allow them to refine you? God wants to make you an expert climber, one who can scale the heights, survive the depths, and in it all, walk in victory.

So let's do it, dear one. Let's be brave and repack our bags with weights that refine.

Five

DISAPPOINTMENT

You have allowed me to suffer much hardship,
but you will restore me to life again and lift
me up from the depths of the earth.

Psalm 71:20

Dis-ap-point-ment: *the feeling of sadness or displeasure caused by*
the nonfulfillment of one's hopes or expectations.[1]

OUR MARRIAGES are particularly vulnerable
when we are disheartened, and unless we're constantly seeking
after the Lord and looking for Him *in* our circumstances, disappointment will become a *distraction*, one that threatens to keep us
from all God has for us. And if we're not careful, the effects of
disappointment can lead to our destruction, steering us away from
our divine appointment to have a strong marriage, bear much
fruit, and live the victorious life.

What about your marriage is disheartening to you today? I
ask you, dear sister, instead of trying to stamp it out, hold it a little
closer. In fact, look straight at your disappointment and say out

loud for your own soul to hear, "My precious Lord is up to something in my life! I will not miss out on what God has for me, because my God is in control. Lord, use my disappointments as a strategy for my life!"

When our anticipation of what we can expect is followed by great disappointment, the pain can be sharp. Here is a portion of an e-mail I received the other day from a friend whose situation is not what she had dreamed of.

> *David,* my husband, hasn't worked in over four years. Because of his illness and chronic pain, I've become the sole provider. I struggle with fear due to health complications, financial ruin, and the threat against a hopeful future. I miss the way my husband used to be. Mostly I suffer from a broken heart, watching the life of the one I love so much suffer in debilitating pain while observing him diminish in strength and vitality. There is simply no area of our lives that his illness hasn't touched or affected.
>
> No day is the same. Every day presents a challenge, and if I stop looking with eyes of faith, I will surely be defeated. The nature of David's illness changes the dynamics of our relationship almost daily. Simply put, David is not always like himself for any number of reasons, and any day he can be different because his pain and strong narcotic medications cause changes to his personality. It is very hard to reconcile and balance between caregiver and the honor of wife, lover, and friend. But I walk on in the power of His sufficient grace. Without the greater relationship with God, I don't know how anyone would endure such a trial. God has promised: "He is close to the brokenhearted and His ears are attentive to their

cry." In spite of everything I still feel so very, very loved. I could not withstand such suffering without the Lord's closeness.

I'm not in denial; I just want to keep faith alive. I know you can't deal with something until you know what it is. You shouldn't imagine the worst. I continue to keep the words of God before me.

For every blow from the Enemy, I've been counteractively blessed by God. No pain has touched us that God hasn't met with a greater measure of His presence.

I want my heart positioned to receive all God has for us, even when the circumstances are difficult. I want to be a catalyst of healing, not a hindrance. I'm waiting, not passively, but in prayer. The Enemy does not have any say over our lives—we belong to God! And He will have the final word. He is the author of this story, and it is not my story, or even our story . . . it is God's!

—Karen from Wisconsin

For her response to this disappointing, one-sided season of marriage, this woman is a modern-day hero. This woman will not be denied; she is holding God to His promises! Reading her story makes me want to slip out of my chair, get on my knees, declare God's goodness, and not relent until His promises come to pass in my life.

We *will* enter into seasons of disappointment. But waiting for us there is a choice that determines if this season will make or break us, empty or empower us. If difficult seasons have the potential for redirecting us, just how do we harness that pain for our greater good? Shouldn't we want to leave our disappointments behind?

□

When we understand that hidden in our disappointments are life lessons, we will view those disappointments as an opportunity to make greater strides in our journey of faith. When we look at disappointments this way, we will be less apt to toss them aside as useless weights that slow us down. Instead, we will hold these seasons closer, knowing they possess the strategy we need for reclaiming what we've lost. And when we believe that God is always up to something in our lives, we will see the value of carrying those afflictions in a different way.

We harness adversity's pain when we embrace this truth: *Every trial that comes our way is measured with grace to carry it and power to be blessed by it.*

Even when our burdens result from our own mistakes, we must not despair. We must repent and face the character flaw that allowed us to stumble, but we must not despair. There is no condemnation for those of us in Christ Jesus. [2]

When we bring everything before the Lord Jesus—our gifts, our flaws, our hopes, our dreams, and the tangled messes we make—God makes something beautiful of our lives. Life is incredibly heavy at times, but God is unfathomably strong. Disappointment can take our breath away, but in due time and at the right time, God will restore our breath, redirect us, *and* put wind in our sails!

When are we redirected by our disappointments? When we see our dreams flapping in the wind, but we confidently reach up and catch the sail! That's when we begin to move. When we determine that God has a *next place* for us, a place of promise and fruitfulness, we will refuse to allow today's disappointments to weigh us down or shipwreck our joy.

Jesus chose you and appointed you to produce fruit, fruit that

□

will last (see John 15:16). The Bible says it is to God's great glory that you become a fruit-bearing, God-fearing, powerful woman of God—one who leaves the earth much better than she found it.

> ## SPIRITUAL LIFT:
> "Beloved, the Spirit of God has come to release you of the effect of dis-appointment. He reminds you, 'Your appointment with your destiny is still set.'"
>
> □ *Francis Frangipane*[3]

A USELESS WEIGHT OR A POWERFUL WEAPON?

The choice we have to continually make is this: Do we embrace our disappointment as a useless weight or a powerful weapon? We will have to carry disappointment at some point in our lives. But will we allow it to weigh us down and weaken our testimony or strengthen us for the greater good?

In other words, will we listen to the thousand voices that tell us we deserve better and are entitled to much more? Or will we allow disappointment to thrust us into a deeper and more intimate place with the Lord? Will we consent to God's dealings with our character and the dross that surfaces when things heat up? And while we are enduring the painful character-refining time, will we still have the courage like the hero in the opening story to *expect* God to be good and big in our midst?

Will we wield this disappointment like a weapon and make the Enemy sorry he ever messed with us? Or will we cling to our lost dreams like a stone life preserver that threatens to pull us under when help is *within our reach?*

It takes great courage to allow the fire to refine you when someone else is guilty of lighting the match. But still, God wastes nothing; and He'll use every injustice, every pain, and every circumstance to make us more like Him (if we let Him). He's especially gentle with the humble, repentant heart; and He's especially tough on the pointing, prideful one.

Pastor J. J. Slag once gave a message that profoundly affected my son. This is my paraphrase of the message as it was relayed to me by my son Luke: "Sometimes when I read the Bible, I stumble over certain passages of Scripture. I see areas in my life where I don't measure up and then I get real uncomfortable. I start to imagine what it would be like to take a little razor and cut out all of the pages that make me feel uncomfortable. Would that make me feel better? Probably not. Then I step back and acknowledge that this is the Word of God I'm holding in my hand. This is God's Word, my Sword. And I realize what I'm actually called to do is to take this Sword and cut everything out of MY life that offends God." [4]

My alone season began six months after I recommitted my life to Christ. Each day after that held new promise and a hope my husband would join me in this faith walk.

Then he told me something I never expected—he didn't believe God existed. The air left my lungs, as if I'd been punched in the stomach.

My heart ached so deeply, I didn't know what to pray.

Scripture tells us, "The Holy Spirit helps us in our weakness. We do not know what we ought to pray for, but the Spirit himself intercedes for us with groans that words cannot express" (Romans 8:26). I believe God allowed me to sense the Holy Spirit to comfort and reassure me of His presence.

Ten years have gone by. I still pray every day for my husband to come to know God, to know His great love and majesty. I still wait. Every day God has blessed our marriage and kept every promise.

I know my husband will one day embrace his Creator, but in the meantime I am free to love him just as he is. God has shown me He doesn't withhold His blessings in such circumstances. He rains them down even more in reward to my faithfulness—to Him and to my husband.

—Dineen from San Jose

Sometimes to survive (and abide) is to completely wrap ourselves around the Vine and hang on for dear life.

When we resolve that we will be Christ followers in every season, something rises up within us and declares that Jesus is Lord of even our circumstances—He is Most High God—high above our perspective—and this is when our disappointment becomes a *direction*.

Let me explain. I am sort of a goal-oriented person. I find real value in getting a vision for my life, my marriage, and my ministry. That way, when I make choices, I am living on purpose.

However, I encountered such frustration when year after year, obstacle after obstacle landed in my path, keeping me from what I thought was God's call and promise on my life. Over and over again, I was frustrated and at a loss with what was happening, wondering if my vision had been all wrong.

For example, deep within my soul was a dream to write, and speak, and help other women come to a place of wholeness and freedom. And yet, every time I took a step in the direction of my "calling," I was faced with reasons I should not be able to do what my heart was telling me to. I lacked time, funds, and ability. Moreover, with every step I took in the direction of my passion, I saw another weakness in my character making me wonder if I would ever be qualified to fulfill my calling.

I watched the news one night, and I was struck by all of the attacks our soldiers encountered while on their way into Afghanistan. Their call was to victory, their goal was the next city, but the immediate skirmishes had to be fought in order to fulfill their call and to get where they were going. This *was* the battle: the skirmishes, the journey, and the next place of victory.

When I began to view the attacks on my life, my marriage, and my call as immediate battles that had to be taken on in order to reach my appointed goal, my disappointments became my direction. In other words, what the Enemy meant for evil served as a divine strategy for me to be blessed for my good and the good of my family.

Instead of the cut-and-run attitude, or even the wishing and whining posture, I decided to press in harder with God to find out why the Enemy was allowed access to my life in this area. Instead of viewing the immediate disappointment as something that would keep me from my destiny, I took it on as something to overcome in order to possess all that God has purposed for me. The Bible says that overwhelming victory is mine in Christ. And I will not be denied. [5]

Here is a tangible example of what I am talking about. When I was a young girl, my warped little mind believed there were two kinds of girls: good ones and bad ones. I figured it had something to do with our DNA. One day I walked into my laundry room to get a change of clothes. I turned around to see my brother's friends leering at me with hungry eyes. I was pinned down and abused by several teenage boys who were looking to satisfy their curiosities.

When I entered the laundry room that day, I believed myself to be a good girl. When I ran out, I felt soiled, believing I must have been wrong and that I wasn't a good girl at all. Because I believed a lie, I allowed the memory of what those boys had stolen from me—a healthy sense of who I was—to return, and, in effect, steal this from me over and over again.

One day when I was walking home from school, I saw these boys' bikes in my front yard. Although I was young, just in elementary school, a determination rose up within me to never let those boys touch me again. I didn't go to my house but walked slowly around and around the baseball diamond, waiting for my mom's car to pull into the driveway.

But suddenly, out of the baseball dugout a different group of boys appeared. They jumped on me. Looking back, I believe they must have been high on something because they laughed wildly as they beat me up, a young girl who was just half their size. They punched me and kicked me, scratched me and pulled my hair. I screamed and wailed but was totally helpless. When they finished, I went home with snarled hair, a swollen lip, and a scratched face.

Jump ahead about twenty-five years. I am married to a solid, strong man and we have three children. My husband and I have both endured one-sided seasons when one of us carried far more than we thought possible. Because of my warped beliefs caused by those childhood experiences, being intimate with Kevin was difficult for me. I saw making love as a chore I endured. If I can be totally honest, I did it out of duty to my husband.

I saw the hurt and disappointment in my husband's eyes because he had a much healthier view of sexuality than I did. He had a right to desire (for both of us) far more than we were experiencing. I came into the marriage feeling defective about my sexuality. Disappointing my husband made me feel even more deficient.

One day during a time of prayer, the Lord revealed to me that Kevin wasn't the only one missing out on a great love life. God also planned for *me* to *enjoy* sexual intimacy with my husband. I almost dismissed the inner voice, because for me it seemed like an impossibility. Yet I couldn't escape the fresh revelation. More and more it nagged me until I realized there was yet another area I had handed over to the Enemy because of ignorance and unbelief.

I began to pray out loud: "In the name of the Lord Jesus, I take back all of the ground I have given over to the Enemy of my soul. I will repossess what is mine now, because God has promised it to me! I take back a thriving, meaningful sex life in Jesus' name! I won't be denied, because I belong to the Most High God who daily fulfills His purposes for me. I thank You by faith, Lord, for a healed, whole, wonderful relationship with my husband. And I will be back tomorrow to pray the same thing until this prayer becomes my reality."

Now to some of you, this may sound a little wild and crazy; but let me tell you, little by little, belief by belief, I got my land back! God gave me a new desire for my husband and He healed the self-hatred in my soul. Do you know how this empowered me? I want it all. I want Jesus to fill, redeem, and restore every lost area of my life.[6] What's especially important about this story is that this was more my husband's disappointment than it was my own. Our sex life would not have been at the top of my list of the losses I grieved during my one-sided season.

Your one-sided, alone season in marriage might include disappointment with your husband or with circumstances you're in because of him. Or maybe it's your husband who is enduring a one-sided season because possibly he has disappointments in you, because of you, or because of circumstances surrounding you. But remember: Whatever the source of the disappointment surrounding you, you have incredible authority and influence in the heavenly realm to pray, to declare the promises of Scripture, and to fight for your treasured one; because that is who your husband is, even if you don't see him that way now or feel like interceding on his behalf.

You must also fight for your own disappointments. Write down the "land" you've handed over because of your unbelief. Ask the Lord to show you corresponding promises from Scripture that are yours to pray and believe for. Do not take this season sitting down! Stand up and fight! All things are possible to you if you will only believe (see Mark 9:23).

□

SPIRITUAL LIFT:

"It is possible, I dare to say, for those who will indeed draw on their Lord's power for deliverance and victory, to live a life in which His promises are taken as they stand, and found to be true."

□ *Rev. Handley C. G. Moule* [7]

Earlier in the chapter I mentioned that Jesus called you to bear a lot of fruit—fruit that will stand the test of time. Well, the rest of that verse goes as follows:

"Then the Father will give you whatever you ask in my name" (John 15:16 NIV).

Abide in Christ amidst your disappointment. Trust in His goodness. Lean on His love. Determine to get His perspective and lean not on your own understanding. Obey Him when He tells you to do something and repent when you are wrong. Walk with Christ every minute of every day. Hold His hand and let Him lead.

Do what He says and listen to the love song He sings over you every single day. Be good to others. Think of practical ways in which you can be good to your husband even if you don't think he deserves it, even if he has disappointed you. Give to those who have less than you do. This is the fruit-bearing life; this is the life that grows branches and juicy fruit from the Vine. This is the life of everyday miracles.

Allow your disappointment to redirect you. Look at your circumstance from a place of victory. You are positioned to reclaim the land. Ask the Father to work on your behalf. He will give you whatever you ask for in His name. "Don't be afraid of the enemy! Remember the Lord, who is great and glorious, and fight for your friends, your families, and your homes!" (Nehemiah 4:14 NLT).

LENDING A HAND

Watch Your Step—Be careful not to surrender to your circumstances. Surrender to God instead. Conceding to your circumstances is like camping in the barren wilderness and forfeiting your dream of something better. Yielding to God *in* your circumstances is to believe that His promises apply to you here; that there is purpose in your pain; and He will come through for you and in due time deliver you.

Stay on the Right Path—Remember, your circumstances don't define you. God does. Don't allow your temporary disappointment to keep you from your divine appointment to bear much fruit, have lots of joy, and experience God's resurrection power *right where you live.*

Run From—Run from the temptation to find your needs met through male friendships. You are better off going without than risking your life, your marriage, the respect of your children and peers, and your reputation. Consider this disappointing season a "fast," and ask the Lord to make up for and fill every empty, barren place. You might even consider a partial fast during this time.[8]

Destination Ahead—Run toward books that fuel your faith and passion for Christ. Spend more time with God. Pray out loud and make heavenly, scriptural declarations over your life. Measure your life against the promises of God, not the perceptions of man. If your reality doesn't line up with what God has promised you, keep walking, keep praying, and keep believing that God is working on your behalf.

Watch the Fine Line—If not tended to, disappointments can fuel depression. Face your disappointments, admit them, and bring them before God; ask Him for a renewed perspective. Take care of yourself during this time; treat yourself to something that nourishes your soul. Be good to yourself. But also understand that you are most vulnerable during times of disappointment. Take the necessary precautions. You know what tempts you; stay away from those things. Spend much time in the Word, and allow your disappointments to fuel your determination and empower you to possess all God has for you.

God's Promise for You Today—"I am still confident of this: I will see the goodness of the LORD in the land of the living" (Psalm 27:13 NIV).

And there's an exhortation for you in the verse that follows: "Wait for the LORD; be strong and take heart and wait for the LORD" (verse 14 NIV).

Holy Father, Precious Friend,

You are all that I need. May my disappointments empower me to live a life of faith. Make this barren land a dance floor where I can twirl, and sing, and relish the fact that I am the object of Your great love. You will come through for me. You will restore my life and redeem every lost thing. This I will declare until I believe it with everything in me: You are for me and not against me, and I will see Your goodness in the land of the living. Thank You, Lord, for being so great that You are high above my circumstances, and for being so near that You are with me in them. My disappointments are redirecting me toward my Promised Land. Oh, how I love You. Amen.

TO THINK ABOUT...

1. Read 2 Corinthians 4:17–18

a. Looking at verse 17, how do you suppose our afflictions can achieve something beautiful—and eternal, no less? Write your thoughts.

b. It's interesting how this verse calls us not to focus on what is seen but what is unseen. And yet, it challenges us to *fix our eyes. . . .* How do you keep yourself from glaring at the problems that are glaring back at you? What are some ways you keep your eternal focus?

2. Read Psalm 68:19, 28

a. Our God is a God who saves, who carries us (and our burdens), and who displays His power at the opportune time. Write down a declarative statement that connects your disappointments with God's willingness to help you.

b. Read verse 28 again. Add to your written statement a heartfelt prayer, asking God to pour out His power and tender mercies in your life. Conclude this written piece

with a prayer of thanks that declares the faithfulness of
God.

3. Read Psalm 30:11–12

a. Take these two verses and expound on the key words
by adding your own words (e.g., *add to mourning,
disappointment*), use a dictionary, a thesaurus, or the
Amplified Bible if you need to. Rewrite your paraphrased
passage into a personalized prayer.

b. Time for listening prayer. Use the above Scripture as a
guideline; allow God to speak to you through this
beautiful passage (e.g., *My Beloved, It is My great delight
to turn your mourning into dancing, and at just the right
time I will . . .*)

4. What is the biggest disappointment you are dealing with
right now? Write it down. Spend a few minutes praying
about this from an "upward perspective." In other words,
begin thanking God, by faith, that He will turn your
disappointment into a dance floor. One way or another,
He'll come through for you if you trust Him. Stay in your
place of prayer until your heart is once again at peace.

Six

LONELINESS

But Jesus often withdrew to lonely places and prayed.

□ Luke 5:16 NIV

I GRABBED a blanket and headed out the door. It frustrated me that my husband's shoulders were so much broader than my own. We were both too busy, but I burned out long before he did. He could carry a commitment until it ran him into the ground and buried him. I didn't have that kind of fortitude. Here I was, burned out and exhausted. And there he was, still forging ahead at a bull's pace, managing another meeting at church, working too many hours every single day.

I walked out on the deck and spotted the love seat. I sat down alone, snuggled with my blanket, and looked up at the sky. For the first few moments, I was numb, and I didn't pay attention to what I was seeing. But then the sky came into focus, and as I looked around me, I was soon blessed.

Puffy white clouds dotted a perfect blue sky. Birds fluttered around and sang songs to one another. Squirrels caught up in a game of tag scurried up and down the trees. The leaves clapped their hands as the breeze blew through their branches.

I was especially taken by the oak. A big gust of wind picked up, and the oak's branches swayed back and forth. But the trunk didn't budge, not even an inch. Years of growth—branches reaching upward and roots growing downward—reflected stability that almost shook me.

God was everywhere. I saw Him in the beautiful sky and in the delight of the birds. I saw Him in the playfulness of the squirrels and the strength of the oak. My backyard became a sanctuary, and I was blessed beyond words to be there.

My kids were at different friends' houses. My husband was gone for the day. So I stayed out in my sanctuary for hours. I took what was sure to have been a lonely, defeating day and recaptured it for a different purpose.

The longer I sat outside and allowed myself to feel the awe that God deserved, the more my soul was nourished and renewed. What a reminder it was for me that when difficult seasons in marriage wound us, extended times in God's presence can heal us.

Before I burned out, I was involved in many things, only a few to which I was called. It's possible that some of my overcommitment was an attempt at keeping the moss from growing on my lonely heart.

Haven't you heard the saying, "Busy women gather no moss"? Okay, I haven't either. Even so, when I finally wore out enough to step back from my many commitments, my loneliness surfaced, and I realized the moss had already begun to grow.

Have you ever realized how a warped sense of empowerment can keep us busy? The busier we get, the more independent we feel. With every un-anointed, un-appointed commitment we make, we place another brick around our hearts. We think that busyness shields us from the loneliness in marriage when in reality it only makes us a prisoner.

Loneliness is a breeding ground for moss. Do you know what moss is? It's a small flowerless green plant that lacks true roots.

Think about that: a small *flowerless* plant that lacks *true roots*. When we are lonely, something grows in our lives; the question (which is utterly dependent on us) is, *What will grow in us?* When confronted with the forlorn face of loneliness, will our spiritual growth produce white flowers of purity that reflect the love of God? Will divine intimacy with our Beloved give off a scent of Christ? Will this season of loneliness in marriage cause our roots to go down deep into His marvelous love?

Or will we grow something of another sort? What will we grow in the valleys, the crevices, the empty places of our hearts? Will we tend to what is growing, or will our distracted hearts be set on "going"?

In other words, will we dig in a little deeper and pay attention to what this loneliness is manifesting in our lives, or will we say of our husbands, "Well, if he's doing *that*, then I'm doing *this*!"? How easy it is to make *his* distraction our license to fill our loneliness as *we* choose! And yet it's at this point where we can miss the appointed route and head down a path of distraction and temptation of our own making.

John the Baptist lived a lonely life. And he understood to whom he belonged. He said this of our heavenly Bridegroom:

The bride belongs to the bridegroom. The friend who attends the bridegroom *waits and listens for him, and is full of joy when he hears the bridegroom's voice.* That joy is mine, and it is now complete. (John 3:29 NIV)

Here is a crucial point: God aches for us when our journey is a lonely one. He understands how painful it is. But He wastes nothing and will often use loneliness to bring *focus* to our lives. John the Baptist was desperately lonely at times, I'm sure. But he allowed God to use his alone time to cultivate a focus and an affection for the One to whom his whole life pointed.

We are the ones who decide how we will let loneliness affect us. Will we choose intimacy with Christ or a shallow identification with the world? Will our loneliness bring sharper clarity about the things of God, or will we miss that blessing and become disoriented with our surroundings?

Your life might be filled with people and conversation and commotion—and you may still be in a season of being lonely. When you feel lonely in marriage, will that loneliness cause you to spend more time in the Lord's company, drawing from Scripture in a deeper way? Or will you squander this time, filling the hours and days with busyness and un-appointed tasks?

Then there is the question of your affections. Will this isolating time bring about a greater loyalty to our one God and Savior, or will you instead fill in the lonely spaces with idols and addictions of this world? This is not to say you shouldn't absolutely pamper yourself when you need it. Treating yourself to a massage, a makeover, or lunch out with friends will definitely lighten your load. Just be careful not to allow a sense of entitlement to lead you into neglecting responsibilities, straying into wrong relationships, or addictive behaviors.

My husband has been on active duty in the U.S. Air Force for fifteen years, twelve of which as a flyer (part of the flight crew). Although he does not usually deploy for long

consecutive periods, he is gone frequently and it all adds up—
we have experienced years where he was gone more than 200
days out of 365. Most of his TDYs (temporary duty) are
between two and three weeks, but sometimes as brief as
overnight or as long as four months at a stretch. I often feel as if I
live out my life on the end of a yo-yo. Even when my husband is
here, his working hours are erratic at best. When I make plans I
have to be prepared to take along the children or find a
babysitter. Family vacations are sometimes cancelled at the last
minute or taken without my husband. But this is the life God
has placed me in, and I have come to, if not love it, be grateful
for what I have and accept His blessings.

There are so many times when I feel weary of filling the
role of a single parent when I'm truly not. Then God whispers:
"To the Lord I cry aloud, and he answers me from his holy hill.
I lie down and sleep; I wake again, because the Lord sustains
me" (Psalm 3:4–5). And my husband is good about calling when
he is away, keeping in touch with me and our sons. We each do
what we can to keep the family together and let the boys know
that they are truly loved, by God even more than by us! Even
when my husband is here, there are times I want to scream in
rage at him for devoting hours to his hobby of music. But then
God reminds me that my husband is home with us and most of
the music he works on is for the church! There are so many other
terrible things a man could be doing; we are blessed to see him
devote his interests to the work of God.

The military life involves a lot of moving, so we do not
have the local community network of family and friends to
sustain us when the going is tough. But God has provided me
with wonderful on-line Christian communities that have

traveled with me wherever I go, a remarkable and emotionally satisfying alternative. God has also provided temporary local friends for my boys wherever we go, and church families where we can serve Him during whatever time He has given us in any specific area. So I have learned to "put (my) hope in God, who richly provides us with everything for our enjoyment" (1 Timothy 6:17). I make it sound easy, perhaps, but it isn't. It's been a long and difficult journey, but I know without doubt that God has been with me every step of the way, and if I keep my eyes on Him, things can only get better!

—Patti, Vogelweh Air Base, Germany

Know that when you are lonely, you are at risk—at risk of being tempted, distracted, and seduced. But instead of this route, you have a great opportunity here. You can choose to recapture your loneliness and use it as a time to reinforce your soul. Extended times in God's presence will deepen your roots and strengthen you to stand. Even Jesus knew the value of withdrawing from the busyness of the day to spend time with His Father.

Depending on how you handle it, loneliness will either build you up or break you down; it will either sharpen the focus of your walk in life or cause you to meander off. Below are a few temptations to avoid during a season of loneliness and distance from your husband.

Temptation 1—SERVE YOURSELF

When loneliness sets in and your needs go unmet by your husband, then comes the desire to meet the needs he is missing *and then some.* Of course, to some degree you have to do for yourself what your husband is not doing for you. For example, your

□

husband may be unavailable for conversation, leaving you to naturally want to talk more often with your girlfriends. We need to
talk, and girlfriends are a gift from God. But if leaning on your
friends takes the place of leaning on God, your spiritual roots will
be shallow and your choices will follow suit.

It's true that if your husband is absent and you're feeling
alone, it can be fun (and very necessary) to get together with girlfriends and eat *this*, buy *that*, or go *there*. But we all know when we
cross over the line to selfishness . . . and that line is different for
every one of us. Be careful with the sense of entitlement that surfaces because of loneliness. You're normal; you're not the only one
who reacts this way; the sense of deserving better surfaces for all of
us. But still, choose well and move forward carefully during this
season and refuse to make choices from that place of entitlement.

Jesus endured times of loneliness and misunderstanding; still,
He cared for the least of these. In our times of loneliness and misunderstanding, He asks us to do the same. Take care of yourself,
but serve the Lord. You are surrounded by people who have it
harder than you, who have less than you, and who could use some
of what God has deposited in you. Ask the Lord to show you who
in your life or sphere of influence needs a cup of water, a hug, a
scented candle, or a prayer. You will be amazed by the supernatural power at work when you serve the Lord instead of yourself. Recapture a servant's heart.

Temptation 2—BUILD A WALL

When we have given our hearts away to our husbands and
find that they are not cared for in a way that makes us feel safe, it
is natural to start building walls. We don't want to be on the receiving end of any more of the disappointment of loneliness, and

we don't want to give what's left of our wounded hearts. This is completely natural and understandable. Boundaries are one thing; walls are another. It's okay to set some healthy boundaries so that you are not swallowed alive by a codependent relationship. But be careful about "protecting" your heart with such hardness that you begin to shut yourself off from the potential for forgiveness, reconciliation, kindness, and love.

The Bible says, "Watch over your heart with all diligence, for from it flow the springs of life" (Proverbs 4:23 NASB). The Lord knows that whatever we allow in and whatever we insist on keeping out will directly affect every aspect of our lives.

But this doesn't mean we tenaciously guard ourselves against potential pain and disappointment. We are called to be at once both tough and tender. Let me explain. We are to be watchful for the lies of the Enemy and tough against any of his attempts to steal from us our sense of identity and purpose and joy. But we are to be tender to the things of God: tender when He corrects us; tender when He calls us to forgive that which we'd rather forget; and tender when He calls us to love—move toward, be kind to— someone we would rather blow off. During the lonely season, resist the temptation to build a wall. Build bridges instead. Reclaim your tender heart.

Temptation 3—LOOK GOOD FOR OTHER MEN

"Stay alert! Watch out for your great enemy, the devil. He prowls around like a roaring lion, looking for someone to devour" (1 Peter 5:8). When you are feeling neglected, overlooked, or incidental, it is completely natural to want to get some of those needs for affection and affirmation met elsewhere. It may be natural, but there is a *super natural* battle going on over this response to your loneliness.

The Enemy of your soul will scheme and arrange scenarios that may massage your ego but threaten your footing. You will run into old flames, potential new flames, or just men who notice what your husband has been overlooking. Don't think for a minute that this is happenstance.

Fighting on the other side of this battle are the heavenly angels who are assigned to your care. The Holy Spirit will arrange divine appointments, words to a song, or the interruption of a child to spare you from the Enemy's seductions. Every day there is an unseen battle going on around us for our souls, our perspectives, and our choices. Someone once said that *we* are the ones who cast the deciding vote as to who wins that battle.

This is not to say that you should let yourself go and stop caring about your appearance. Exercise, eat right, get dressed for the day, and put a comb through your hair, but do these things for the right reasons. Love yourself; love who God is making you to be. Stay on your path; keep your eyes fixed on Jesus. Be your best because you are blessed with a Savior who loves you and wants the best of everything for you! Renew your commitment to purity.

Temptation 4—CREATE A DIFFERENT REALITY

When our reality is less than appealing, it is very tempting to engage in an activity that helps us escape for a time from our current circumstances. Some women spend hours reading racy novels, watching soap operas, and chatting on cyberspace. Please hear my heart. I am not trying to get legalistic on you. One of my favorite things to do is to curl up with a good novel. But the Holy Spirit will let us know when the things we are doing dishonor Christ, when we are looking to those wrong things to fill in what is really going wrong in our lives.

Do you have a *thing*? What's the thing you're using to fill in your lonely season in marriage? Are you defensive when someone questions your "other reality"? Can you lay it down for a season and seek the Lord in a deeper way? Ask Him to renew and restore your reality as it should be—found in Him. He can make your life something you cherish and embrace. Begin to pray Scripture. Ask God to give you a picture of what "above and beyond all I could ever dare to ask or dream" would look like in your life (see Ephesians 3:20).

A word about a few of the things I mentioned above. Racy novels (the ones that describe sexual acts and unrealistic relationships) will only serve to lead you away from your faith, create expectations that your spouse can never live up to, and open up your mind to literal temptations with other men. Regarding soap operas, I think they are a waste of your valuable time; but that's between you and the Lord. Using chat rooms to cultivate a relationship with the opposite sex is dangerous, unwise, and incredibly risky behavior. If you need more companionship than you're currently experiencing, join a prayer/support group with a few godly women. Guard your heart; guard your life! Repossess your reality!

Temptation 5—NEGLECT YOUR HUSBAND

When you feel neglected, it's easy to return the favor. I never set out to pay him back, but as I mentioned at the beginning of the book, during our tough season I (somewhat unconsciously) gave Kevin the bumpy pillow, the small piece of chicken, and I was even tempted to wash his white underwear with my son's red soccer socks.

Okay, maybe I'm being really open about my glaring faults; maybe you never feel tempted to overcook his steak or undercook his noodles. But do search your heart to find out if there is any area where you have stopped caring for your husband in the way the Lord would ask of you. The upward call on this journey is the call to love our husbands . . . so love him. Jesus said, "I tell you the truth, when you refused to help the least of these my brothers and sisters, you were refusing to help me" (Matthew 25:45). Replenish your marriage!

SPIRITUAL LIFT:

"It is easy to love the people far away. It is not always easy to love those close to us. It is easier to give a cup of rice to relieve hunger than to relieve the loneliness and pain of someone unloved in our own home. Bring love into your home, for this is where our love for each other must start."

□ *Mother Teresa*[1]

Temptation 6—HAVE A WILD THOUGHT LIFE

Jesus said, "Where your treasure is, there your heart will be also" (Matthew 6:21 NIV). When we lose sight of the treasure we have in Christ, our thoughts take on a life of their own! Women in one-sided seasons have spoken to me about their temptations to fantasize about other men, or about being alone (and not having to deal with their husbands), about living someone else's life, and about different ways to alleviate the pain they feel.

It is difficult to keep a fresh and fruitful thought life alive when the moments of our everyday lives blend together with no apparent sign of change. Beth Moore wrote:

> We reach for the fruit of forbidden trees because we're getting a little bored with a steady diet of nothing but apples and bananas. Some of us haven't widened our spiritual horizons in decades. We are doing exactly the same things to fuel our Christian faith that we did years ago, and we're in a rut. A spiritual rut is fertile ground for seduction. . . . An unsatisfied soul, an empty abyss, is nothing but a stronghold waiting to happen.[2]

I always say, "When we don't allow our thoughts to run wild, they will run deeper." We must guard our thoughts like we guard our hearts. Our victories and defeats always begin in our thoughts. The Bible does say that we will be transformed when we renew our minds (see Romans 12:2). I devote a whole chapter to our thought lives in my book *Balance That Works When Life Doesn't*. I pray you'll read it someday.

In the meantime, pay attention to your thoughts every single day. Practice catching yourself each time your mind wanders off track to places you know it shouldn't go and bring it back. Memorize this prayer: "In Jesus' name, I refuse any thought that weakens or distracts me. I will take all of my thoughts captive and make them obedient to Christ. My mind will be a place where Christ's glory dwells!" Reinforce a holy, healthy mind-set!

Temptation 7—LIVE IN THE SHALLOWS

When we live in the shallows, being convicted of our selfish attitudes, unforgiveness, and halfhearted faith has less and less of an impact on us. But when we follow Christ to the depths of His love and calling on our lives, those ungodly things become difficult, if not impossible, to hang on to.

The presence of God is unsettling for those who pretend. The most miserable people on earth are those who have one foot in the kingdom and one foot in this world. But when we walk closely with the Lord, He deals with our character, calls us higher, and calls us deeper. When we are willing to go to those deep places with God, He entrusts us with the great honor of being used by Him in powerful ways. But He continues to keep accountability a primary factor and He does this for our safety.

As soon as we make a departure in our minds, we open ourselves up to seduction of every kind. God deals with us, and His ways might seem harsh at times, but He is only extracting from our lives that which will destroy us if we open ourselves up to the wiles of the Enemy.

Spend some of your prayer time being quiet and listening to God. Ask Him to point out anything in you that offends Him (see Psalm 139:23–24). Some of the deterrents to a deeper life are busyness, unbelief, and a refusal to look inward. Are you busy, distracted, or afraid? Still waters run deep. Carve out time to be still and reflect on the love God has for you. This will cultivate in you a hunger and a thirst for a more peaceful life. Replace the shallows with a deeper life in Christ!

During a lonely season in marriage—when the person who should be your best friend and companion is not near you for whatever reason—it's especially tempting to find companionship in overcommitment, unhealthy habits, or wrong relationships. Refuse to let the Enemy pollute your life! Do you have loneliness in your life bag right now? Carry it with the grace that God supplies. Recapture those lonely times and replenish your soul by spending time in God's presence.

LENDING A HAND

Watch Your Step—Be careful not to think too highly of your ability to withstand temptation during this lonely season. You're safest when you walk in the fear of the Lord (see Proverbs 19:23; 29:25).

Stay on the Right Path—Remember to recapture your lonely times for your soul's sake! Reinforce your walk of faith with worship, prayer, and time in God's Word. Enjoy God's creation; look for your river in this desert! Look for the ways God is showing up to bless you. Count your blessings, not your lonely days. Remember how He's been faithful; determine to believe He'll come through for you again.

Run From—Run from the tendency to satisfy your desires with garbage and time wasters. You are far too valuable for that! Run from the temptation to flirt with other men. Only plant seeds in your own garden. Take sides against yourself if you have to, and walk away from tempting opportunities. Walk in the Spirit and you will not satisfy the desires of the flesh (see Galatians 5:16).

Destination Ahead—Run toward women friends who challenge your faith and tell you the truth. Run toward an accountability partner. Use this time to become stronger both physically and spiritually. Daily proclaim, "Greater is He that is in me than he that is in the world!"

Watch the Fine Line—Don't allow this lonely season to draw you away from people and church involvement. Stay in the game! But be careful about getting too overcommitted. Don't be busy for the sake of staying busy. Make sure you are investing in the things God has appointed for you. There will be days when you're called to run, and days when you're called to rest. Don't be afraid of those moments when He slows you down and you feel that ache in your heart. He will meet you there.

God's Promise for You Today—"No temptation has seized you except what is common to man. And God is faithful; he will not let you be tempted beyond what you can bear. But when you are tempted, he will also provide a way out so that you can stand up under it" (1 Corinthians 10:13 NIV).

Sovereign Lord,

I know Your heart aches with mine. I know You are with me on this journey. I ask for Your mercy right now. Lead me not into temptation; deliver me from evil. Hide me in the shadow of Your wings during my vulnerable moments. The Enemy would love to see me fall, but You want me to flourish! Reinforce me, Lord; help me to thrive in this desperate place. Take my sinful, selfish tendencies and replace them with a passion and a conviction to follow hard after You. I will trust You and I will not be afraid. May this lonely time turn into a

□

retreat of solitude and a time of strengthening. May Your presence be so real, and Your Word so rich that I find myself spending hours with You. May my life bear fruit from this place for years to come. I am Yours, Lord. Amen.

TO THINK ABOUT...

1. Read Psalm 25:16–18, 20–21

a. This passage addresses loneliness; it is a cry for help, but also a request for forgiveness. Write out your own prayer asking for God's help *and* forgiveness. Be specific.

b. Notice how verses 20 and 21 speak of being protected from without and strengthened from within. List some tangible ways you need God's protection from temptations, etc. List some areas in your character you sense God wants to strengthen.

2. Read Psalm 121

Though your husband may be distracted, and you may feel alone, the Lord is near and attentive to every detail of your life. Verse 1 asks a question, verse 2 answers it; verses 3 through 8 describe God's provision and intervention in your life. Write out numbers 1 through 8 in the left margin, and next to each number, describe the question, the answer, and the provision, and how each relates to your specific situation. Take your time; savor the flavor; the Bible is a powerful gift!

b. Which promise stands out most to you today? Explain.

He's always watching over me + will keep me from harm.

□

3. Read 1 Samuel 12:21–22

a. Rewrite these verses into a personalized declarative statement. Once you're done, read it out loud and determine to do and believe what it says!

b. Before you move into your time of listening prayer, read Psalm 139:23–24 and pray those verses. Wait silently in God's presence until you're ready to write . . . then begin with, "Precious one, I want you to know that I . . . "

4. The unfailing love of the Lord surrounds the one who trusts in Him (see Psalm 32:10). He has you on all sides. Refuse to let loneliness swallow you whole. Harness the lonely moments and bring yourself before your Maker. Ask for an increased capacity to know and embrace the love that surrounds you. Write a prayer that's on your heart today.

3.A. Don't look to idols. Keep your mind on God. You are His Child.

Seven

IMPERFECTION

God—He clothes me with strength
and makes my way perfect

He makes my feet like the feet of a deer
and sets me securely on the heights.

Psalm 18:32–33 HCSB

ONCE WHEN my husband and I were having a spat, I looked at him, narrowed my eyes, and said, "Even though I'm wrong most of the time, that doesn't make you better than me!" He started to laugh, which really bugged me. But then I started to laugh too. Truly, his strengths are my weaknesses, and even though my strengths are his weaknesses, I am most bothered by my own imperfections.

We are made for the climb. God continually calls us upward. Even in the low places and the valleys of life, Jesus leads us to the highest ground. The tough thing about the upward climb, though, is that with each new level to which we aspire, we are confronted with a new degree of weakness within us. That's why most people would rather camp in the valley than climb up a mountain.

Marriage is a climb, and it has a way of exposing the best and worst of who we are. The road gets long and the hills are high, and all too often our weaknesses and inadequacies present themselves on our journey, even ones we thought we conquered miles ago. We can be, or think we are, defeated at times.

When we look in our backpack and are forced to reckon with all of the imperfections we carry, aren't we weakened because of them? Aren't we happiest on the strong days? Isn't it better to tuck our imperfections in one of those side pockets and close the zipper? How exactly do our imperfections establish us?

Let's look at the athlete for a little insight.

Athletes face their personal weaknesses all day long. In order to get stronger, they lift weights that are too heavy for them. This actually *breaks down* the muscle. After the muscle repairs itself, you have a stronger muscle. In order for athletes to increase their speed, they run so hard their lungs burn; this is not fun. And yet, by repeatedly asking their bodies to push beyond what's comfortable, they achieve a greater measure of strength and fitness.

Because of the training they have been doing, athletes in prime condition can respond to a sudden physical demand without landing themselves in traction. An athlete can do what the average person cannot. But their abilities didn't come overnight and without hard work. No matter what anyone says, you cannot take shortcuts and get instant, miraculous results from a pill advertised in the latest infomercial.

You are being conditioned to scale new heights. You are being trained for battle. God wants to use every aspect of your life (even your marriage) to refine you. This requires that you take total inventory of what you are carrying. You were not born to watch from the sidelines. You were not made for shortcuts. You were born, called, and equipped to make a difference in your world, in your community, and in the heart of your family.

As you make your way on this journey, you will be asked to

climb higher, give more, and forgive more than you would prefer. Sometimes you will feel your muscles strain, your lungs burn, and your patience tried to its limits. You will have days when you are tempted to totally despair because of the weakness and inadequacy you see in yourself. You may fall down in a heap, full of self-contempt and refuse to take another step. That's okay—as long as you eventually get up and take another step.

You will be stretched in marriage. You will be challenged beyond your ability and desire. You will see things in your spouse and yourself that completely dishearten you. You will speak and react in ways that will later make you cringe.

We didn't have a choice. Who would have chosen a malignant brain tumor? One day we got up and our lives would never be the same, never. Surgery confirmed my husband's brain tumor, an aggressive one. Doctors gave him at the most six months to live, but God had other plans.

After a year and a half of radiation and chemotherapy treatment, the condition was healed; we were supposed to get back to "normal." This new "normal" included his difficulty storing new memories. They seemed to get lost in his brain. Damaged hormone levels and trauma made our intimate lives almost nonexistent.

I became angrier with each passing day. I wondered why God didn't heal his memory, his hormones, or his personality, which had become quite different. I knew God was big enough, but it was as if God withheld the things that mattered to me. Many times I would ask WHY?

117

Life had to go on. I didn't have time to find an answer; besides, God wasn't answering. Plus, every time the little WHY word came up, my guilt was overwhelming. How dare I ask WHY when my husband had been divinely healed?

Years went by before God clearly said, "You need to marry this man." *This man*, I thought. Haven't we been married for the past sixteen years?

I knew God was saying the man I married years before had died and with him went my commitment. In that case, I wasn't so sure I wanted to marry this man. Things had gotten quite hard, and I was tired of it all.

After months of wrestling with God, I finally surrendered. In December that year, with hands shaking worse than the first time, I stood before God and made a vow to stand beside this man through sickness and health, knowing firsthand what those words meant.

What I have learned is this: Real commitment is for a lifetime, and it means sticking it out through the thick and the thin. I learned that obedience to God is much more important than getting my way.

As for why, God has used all of this to transform me into the person He wants me to be, a person able to minister to others with compassion and grace.

Now my faith is growing. I am believing the miracle-working God can restore what sickness, trauma, and change has taken away and continue healing our relationship. We have seen that God is always able to compensate for whatever is lacking. He is ever faithful.

—Denise from Georgia

I remember a time when I told Kevin that since he was gone so much, I had learned to live without him. But that wasn't true. I was speaking in anger. I missed him and I ached over our lack of togetherness. He was hurt by my words, and I couldn't take those words back.

How are we supposed to live with ourselves, being quite aware of our glaring imperfections?

Being established and strengthened while carrying the weight of our imperfections takes a large measure of grace and understanding. Many people like to pretend they are carrying no imperfections with them. They emphasize all of their good points and hide their not-so-good points in the bushes next to the poison ivy.

But God doesn't let us off the hook that easily. He knows that facing our imperfections will create dependence, and dependence creates fruitfulness, and fruitfulness brings Him much glory. Furthermore, when we take this walk of faith seriously and determine to stay close to Jesus, we will be perfected by becoming more and more like Him. Not that we bear fruit by focusing on fruit; we bear fruit by focusing on Him.

You see, Jesus *is* patience; Jesus *is* peace; He *is* love, joy, faithfulness, and goodness. And when you hang around with Joy, you eventually become Joy-full. When you spend time with Patience, you can't help but reflect patience to others.

We first came to Jesus because of our need. We were bound for hell because of our sin and selfish state. We needed Jesus' perfect and unselfish love to save us. And now that we're saved, we daily need His life to be at work in and through us.

So how do our imperfections repeatedly establish us? They remind us of our need; they keep us from venturing off too far on our own; they bring us back to the cross; and they keep us on our knees. In our weakness He is strong. We are most strong when we are most aware of our need and most connected to the Source of our strength.[1]

Our call is to *holy confidence and humble dependence*: We are to walk through life with our heads high, knowing it is Jesus who loves us and qualifies us for His purposes. We have no reason to look down. But our confidence must remain closely linked with our humble dependence.

With God, we can accomplish mind-boggling things, but the higher we climb, the more important it is to remember that we can fall from any level. We have all sadly seen this happen with people in high-profile ministries. And we risk falling when we begin to look at ourselves, trust in ourselves, and believe that we have ownership of our gifts. Humble dependence that comes from acknowledging our imperfections is our safety harness. We began our journey admitting our need, and we will be victorious if we continue on the way we started.

Let me put this question to you: How did your new life begin? Was it by working your heads off to please God? Or was it by responding to God's Message to you? Are you going to continue this craziness? For only crazy people would think they could complete by their own efforts what was begun by God. If you weren't smart enough or strong enough to begin it, how do you suppose you could perfect it? (Galatians 3:2–3 THE MESSAGE)

It's a paradox, really. We are most powerful, most effective, and the greatest threat to the Enemy of our souls when we understand that we are both *nothing* and *everything*. We are nothing *without* Jesus, but we are everything *to* Him. We can do all things,

□

SPIRITUAL LIFT:

"Our deficiencies are more than made up for by the Holy Spirit. God can and will make up the shortfall in our lives. God stands in our credibility gap and smiles. He stands in our hypocrisy and gives us legitimacy. And He does it gladly!"

□ *Graham Cooke*[2]

survive all things, and climb every mountain with the Lord Jesus by our side.

No matter what state our marriage is in right now, and no matter who's at fault, we must reckon with our own imperfections (and yet not be threatened by them). We can learn to joyfully walk in the humble knowledge that though we have far to go, *we've come far*, and though our sins are many, *they are washed in the blood*, and though we may blow it tomorrow, *Jesus has already gone ahead to make provision for us.*

When we fall down because of our imperfections, we get up. We accept forgiveness and we embrace gratitude for the gift of a new beginning. This is what it means to be reestablished. You're never more secure than just after you've blown it because your memory of sin, forgiveness, and grace are right on your shoulder.

Your certain mistrust of self keeps you clinging to the Vine. And your desire to walk blamelessly before God is renewed.

We are actually strengthened when we admit we are weak! What a powerful paradox! What freedom it is to know *who we are*—the good, the bad, and the ugly—and with that knowledge, walk joyfully on our way. We are not full of ourselves because we know how capable we are of sin. But we refuse self-deprecation because we were made in the image of God.

As you stumble along the way through your alone season in marriage, and you fumble the ball, miss the mark, or speak without thinking, don't wait! Get yourself before the Lord right away. Confess your sin and acknowledge your need for more of Christ in you. Ask for forgiveness. Then *make yourself smile* because you have a place to go with your foibles.

Joe and I had married quite young—nineteen years young, in fact. We did everything together. We moved around the country with his work, and, not knowing anyone in each new location, we could only depend on each other. We attended churches, but each was a temporary situation, since we would be moving on in a few weeks or months. After a few years of our vagabond lifestyle, our oldest child became school-aged, and that was the end of our moving every few months.

We settled in our country home and built a life many miles away from my family and Joe's. We still did everything together, though. We built a business, attended a local church, and made friends. The years passed, and our children graduated from school, then went to college, and soon left home to build their careers. Once again, it was just Joe and me.

Like many couples, we discovered that during the busy

years of raising children we had grown apart. Joe had been consumed with work, and I was preoccupied with children and the home. We worked on rebuilding our relationship and learning who we were apart from the children.

During the time of adjusting to an empty nest, I received the call that my mother had been diagnosed with inoperable, terminal cancer. Thus began two heart-wrenching years of ups and downs until her eventual death. During that time, Joe seemed to enter a midlife crisis. He became panicky and depressed and turned into a near stranger. My conservative husband suddenly wanted to learn how to dance, go to country music bars, play the saxophone, and take flying lessons. He was seldom home—but when he was physically, mentally he was elsewhere—and all this came at a time when I desperately needed a strong, compassionate man by my side. It was not to be, and I was on my own.

God was about to teach me a hard lesson. Only when the people I depended on most were removed from me did I come to the truth—that God is the source of my life. God is the One who provides strength and comfort. He is the One who provides joy and peace inside me in the middle of any storm.

I can't say God struck our lives with a sudden bolt of lightning and everything is perfect now. It certainly isn't, but I can say that I am a stronger woman, a wife and mother who truly learned who her help comes from and that with God's help, I can stand and survive the storms of life.

Psalm 121:2—"My help comes from the Lord, the Maker of heaven and earth."

—Ann from the Midwest

Give yourself permission to be human. But remind yourself that you are made for another world. God wants to redeem every area of your life. He's preparing you for eternity, which means He wants you to be less human today than you were last year. "He must increase, but I must decrease" (John 3:30 HCSB).

If you continue this walk of faith and forgiveness, in a year from now you will be able to say, "I am stronger. I am more fit for the climb. I understand forgiveness in a deeper way. And I have a greater capacity to love today than I did yesterday."

Below is one of my favorite poems, written by Rev. J. C. Lavater in the 1800s.

> *O Jesus Christ, grow Thou in me,*
> *And all things else recede;*
> *My heart be daily nearer Thee,*
> *From sin be daily freed.*
> *Make this poor self grow less and less*
> *Be Thou my life and aim;*
> *Oh, make me daily, through Thy grace,*
> *More worthy of Thy name.*[3]

LENDING A HAND

Watch Your Step—Be careful when the way is steep. Determine not to make "big decisions" during the uphill seasons. Don't despair when your weaknesses surface; just declare where your strength comes from. This is not a cliché; this is a powerful declaration when made by faith. Say out loud, "My strength comes from the Lord! He loves me, forgives me, accepts me, and leads me onward!" You'll feel your strength grow!

Stay on the Right Path—Remember to pace yourself. When life gets so strained that you begin seeing your imperfections everywhere (even ones that are not real), you know it's time to pitch your tent beside the still waters and ask the Lord to restore your soul (see Psalm 23). You are made for great exploits, but you also need a nap once in a while.

Run From—Run from what C. S. Lewis calls "diseased introspection." Don't spend time mulling over your imperfections (or your husband's, for that matter). Several minutes of this, and you've opened your life up to a self-centered, self-defeating stronghold. Refuse to allow the accuser to walk along the path with you. Too often, we wave off those harassing thoughts like gnats that keep coming back when what we need to do is stop, put our foot down, and command any enemy of Jesus to get off our path!

Destination Ahead—Run toward the love of God, every single day. Remind yourself, on the hour if you have to, that you are the object of God's love. Don't be surprised when your flaws and foibles surface; these things cannot keep you from your destiny unless you let them. Bring the slightest departure to the Lord. Every slighting thought, every negative emotion—bring it to Him and ask for His peace and perspective instead.

Watch the Fine Line—Relish the love of God, but remember that He is serious about our sin. Refuse to minimize or explain away your bad behaviors and attitudes (even if your husband's issues seem like a mountain to your molehill). God is intent on extracting from your life everything that is contrary to His nature. Rise up in confidence with each new day because His fresh, new mercies are waiting just for you. But as one of my mentors always says, "Before you rise up, first, bow down." We need Jesus every hour.

☐

God's Promise for You Today— "The one thing I ask of the Lord—the thing I seek most—is to live in the house of the Lord all the days of my life, delighting in the Lord's perfections and meditating in his Temple. For he will conceal me there when troubles come; he will hide me in his sanctuary. He will place me out of reach on a high rock. Then I will hold my head high above my enemies who surround me" (Psalm 27:4–6).

Precious Lamb of God,

You are the faithful One. Even when I am faithless or forgetful, You never are. Help me not to get hung up on my imperfections; for they remind me of my need for You! Forgive me when I behave in ways that don't honor You. Take me to the higher place You have for me. I want to climb every mountain You've assigned to be under my feet. I will trust You and I will count on Your forgiveness. Help me to be brave in the face of my imperfections; acknowledging them and looking to You establishes me. Heighten my conviction to walk in holiness, humility, and love. I need You every moment of the day. Fill me anew this day. Amen.

TO THINK ABOUT...

1. Read Ephesians 3:14–15

a. Try this once. Kneel down before the Lord. Tell Him how mighty and awesome and wonderful He is. Spend a few moments declaring His greatness from your humble position.

b. Take a moment and write down your thoughts about what that was like for you.

2. Read Ephesians 3:16–19

a. Read this passage again slowly; it is packed with promise. Out of His abundance, He wants to do great things in and for *you*. List some of those things based on the passage you have just read. . . .

b. The only way we can take hold of all God has for us is to put more confidence in His goodness than we do our "bad-ness." Though our sin must be confessed, we are always promised forgiveness. Write out a prayer that acknowledges your imperfections and needs, but that also *emphasizes* Christ's amazing love and strength.

3. Read Ephesians 3:20

a. Write this wonderful verse into a personalized prayer.

b. Now use this same verse as a guide for your listening prayer.

4. God knows you fully and loves you deeply. Trust His opinion of you more than you do your own thoughts and perspective of your imperfections. Memorize 2 Corinthians 10:5 and recite it every time negative thoughts of imperfections threaten to overtake you.

Eight

WAITING

*But the Lord still waits for you to come to him so he can show
you his love and compassion. For the Lord is a faithful God.
Blessed are those who wait for him to help them.*

Isaiah 30:18 NLT

HANNAH LEANED against the old, dead tree
and stared off into space. With one hand on her womb and the other
on her face, she forced back the tears that threatened to flow. She
whispered under her breath, "How long, O Lord, until I see a breakthrough?" She hadn't eaten in days because the ache in her heart
overshadowed any desire for food.

She squeezed her eyes shut as a heavy breeze blew dust in her
in face. A couple of tears escaped and made clean trails as they
trickled down her cheeks. She was startled when two hands
touched her shoulders. Her husband wrapped his arms around her
and pulled her close. "What's the matter, Hannah?" he asked.
"Why aren't you eating? Why be so sad because you have no children? You have me—isn't that better than having ten sons?"

Hannah turned to face her husband and looked into eyes that
could never understand her shame, her unfulfilled desire, and the

pain of being constantly taunted and misunderstood. She buried her head in his chest and swallowed her pain one more time.

After dinner one night, Hannah went to church to pray to the Lord. She was in deep anguish and she cried bitterly. She poured out her heart to her Savior and cried these words, "O Lord Almighty, if you will look down upon my sorrow and answer my prayer and give me a son, then I will give him back to you. He will be yours for his entire lifetime . . . " (Read 1 Samuel 1)

Does *waiting* feel like a heavy burden in your life bag right now? How long have you been journeying, waiting to see things change? Are you in a season of marriage where, if you let yourself, you'd bury your head in a pillow and just cry the afternoon away? Do you struggle with thoughts that betray your marriage? Do you wonder what to do with all of your betraying thoughts? Perhaps you've asked yourself these questions: *Will it always be like this? What if he doesn't change?*

Hannah was a woman in waiting. She was waiting for a breakthrough, waiting for a promise; she was waiting on the Lord. Not only did Hannah live with the emptiness of an unfulfilled dream, she was taunted and harassed by a jealous woman who daily reminded her of her shame.

When you read Hannah's story, what ache or longing comes to your mind? Surely you understand what it's like to have an unfulfilled dream. Some of you grasp the soul-filled pain Hannah lived with every single day. Hannah ached for her dream to be fulfilled. But instead of taking things into her own hands, she took her request directly to the Lord. Hannah cried out to God for all she was worth, and she committed the outcome to Him.

Year after year, Hannah's rival provoked and harassed her until she was too upset to eat. Year after year, Hannah watched others give birth to their dreams while she waited for her own breakthrough. Hannah didn't run from God; she ran to Him, and in due time, her prayers were answered.

I don't know if I would have the fortitude to keep the promise Hannah made to God, but she did. Hannah promised that if God would bless her with a son, she would give him back to the Lord, and that's exactly what she did. As soon as Samuel was weaned, she took him to the house of the Lord. Listen to Hannah's words: "I prayed for this child, and the LORD has granted me what I asked of him. So now I give him to the LORD. For his whole life he will be given over to the LORD" (1 Samuel 1:27–28 NIV).

I mention this part of Hannah's story because it reminds me of something pastor and author Francis Frangipane once said. He said, "The believer's life will always be one of conquering and surrendering."[1]

In other words, we are called to conquer and possess the promises God has made available to us, and then we must bow low and humbly thank Him and then surrender our victories back to Christ, from whom they have come. We take hold of that which He has promised us, we raise the victory flag and declare that no one who trusts in the Lord will ever be put to shame (Psalm 25:3), and then we give our treasures back to Him.

As you wait on the Lord, as you look to Him for a breakthrough in your marriage, prepare your heart for humble surrender. Whenever you see a positive change in your husband, don't cling to it; don't even cling to him, but cling to God instead. Repeat Hannah's words when speaking of your husband, "For his whole life he will be given over to the Lord." Return your victories to

God; hold your husband's life and character with an open hand, and see what the love of God will do.

—————

What does Hannah's story have to do with waiting, especially in the context of marriage? After all, she was married to a good man, right? Wasn't hers a struggle to conceive and not a problem in her marriage?

Her story has everything to do with you.

Do you feel that flutter of life in your spirit? Even if you feel nothing, God is up to something. He has planted a seed of something beautiful in you. You have unfulfilled longings in your life, you have dreams you may be afraid to admit, and you have a God who is infinitely good. You may have a strong marriage, you may have a weak one; but either way, you are in a season when you need a breakthrough. And you've come to the right place because God specializes in the desires of our heart.

Not to say that He gives us everything we want. He gives us more than that. He promises us life eternal and His presence here on earth. He promises healing, restoration, deliverance, and divine intervention wherever we allow Him to move. He cares about our smallest desires; and while our character and Christlikeness is of utmost importance to Him and He will deal with our sin, He still does the sweetest things for us every single day.

Have you thought of the time of waiting as a gift? Without the gift of waiting, where would our expectation be? Though it feels heavy to carry, if we shift our weight and carry it with the strength God provides, all of our waiting moments *can* serve to renew us. Waiting can actually fuel us to expect more from God; and it pleases Him greatly when we press in, seek, pray, and take hold of all of the things He so lovingly longs to give.

As you lean into the arms of your Beloved and shift your burdens there, you will find everything for which your soul longs. You will eventually lay down expectations that are not from Him. You will gain clarity about the things God wants to give you. You will find a flutter of faith in your spiritual womb and a fresh, new hope in your heart. And for every waiting moment you bring before the Lord, you will be assured that God works for those who wait for Him; He blesses those who wait for Him, and He longs to birth something new in your life. [2]

Your heavenly Father says to you . . .

I've planted a seed in the womb of your soul,
A dream for your life, for a heart that is whole
It's moving within taking shape as you grow
Walk on in faith, because you're starting to show.
Others will notice and say, "Your promise, it comes!"
The timing is Mine, not yours, I'm the One
Who decides how to bring your promise to you
So trust Me and wait, believe My Word, for it is true
As the life of your dream takes shape in your soul
Lean into the arms of the One who knows
The place, the day, and the time of release
Say to the world, "God knows what's best for me!"
Let's wait together in joyful expectation
Not grasping or striving for an early celebration
The world needs a dream prepared through and through
When you wait on the Lord, all of Heaven establishes you

*My beloved, I am birthing something wonderful in you . . .
wait for Me.*[3]

It's difficult to wait. Especially when we are rigid, frustrated,
and counting the minutes until something changes. Waiting like
this can make us sick and give us wrinkles (I'm convinced of this).
There must be a better way, right?

I've talked with many women who are in waiting: waiting for
their husbands to work less or work more or just plain work. I've
listened to women share the ache in their hearts as they wait for
their husbands to take the spiritual leadership of the home, while
other women say they would do victory laps if only their husbands believed.

Due to my husband's abuse of alcohol, I felt alone
throughout most of my forty-two-year marriage. Some people
ask, "How did you do it? Why did you stay?"

I went through many emotions over the years—anger,
disappointment, hopelessness, helplessness. Many people would
have applauded my decision if I had chosen to get out of the
marriage.

Early on, I became profoundly aware of my need to have a
deeper relationship with Jesus. I knew, too, that I had to be strong
spiritually in order to influence our children for Christ. I got
involved in church ministry and attended with our three children,
but mostly alone. Although my husband was raised in the church
and had even attended a Christian school, he now attended
church only once in a while, and then mostly for social reasons.
The spiritual guidance of the family was my responsibility.

A vital part of my growth was being a part of a group of

Christian women who supported me and were a positive influence in my life, as well as reading my Bible, praying, and listening to inspirational speakers. One of the key principles I discovered during my journey through the alone years was that I could ask God to love my husband through me when I felt I couldn't do it myself.

We went through the hard time of losing our business. At age sixty, we were penniless and panicking. Yet God used this and many other circumstances to renew our marriage. I am so grateful for God's amazing grace. We are now reading the Bible together and joyfully attending a church that we love. God opened doors for my husband to be in an occupation that he loves and is gifted at! Most wonderful of all has been a gradual transformation in the heart of my husband and a deeper faith, peace, and joy than I have ever experienced! Even though I made mistakes and it was hard work, I'm so glad I listened to God's leading and didn't get out of the marriage. We are enjoying our children and grandchildren together!

—Donna from Idaho

Some women are waiting for a breakthrough in finances, others for a break from the constant despair of depression. Still others are just waiting for a break—a break from the exhausting, day-to-day demands of caring for a home without their husband's support.

One woman told me, "First I was waiting for my husband to change. God is a God of change. As my husband matures, he will change . . . right? So I waited. At some point, my waiting changed to waiting on God; waiting on Him to meet my needs; waiting on Him to change me."

□

The heavens are pregnant with promise. God wants to establish us as a people who know Him well enough to trust Him and wait for Him. The problem is, we are so busy grabbing for ourselves, we never give God a chance to give us His best.

When Kevin, my husband, was very sick, we received loads of phone calls, cards, and e-mails. All of these things were a huge source of encouragement to us. One e-mailed story especially blessed and challenged me. It went something like this:

A little girl had her eye on a set of pearls she had spotted in the toy store window. She worked and saved and worked and saved until she had enough money to purchase the pearls. She was so captivated by the pearls that she didn't want to part with them; she even took them to bed with her. One night the girl's dad came to tuck her in bed. He sat down beside her, tucked a tuft of hair behind her ear and asked, "You still sleeping with those pearls? Can I have them?"

She loved her daddy, but she also cherished her new pearls. She looked in his eyes, clutched her pearls a little tighter, and pulled them to her chest. Her father spoke up. "That's okay, honey. I love you." Then he pulled up her covers, kissed her head, and told her to sleep well.

Night after night the dad mentioned the pearls and asked to have them, and each night the little girl paused a little longer because she loved her dad so very much. Finally, after about five nights of this, the girl closed her eyes and handed over the pearls, still not wanting to see them go. Just as quickly her father pulled out a set of genuine pearls and placed them in her hand. He again kissed her head and said, "I love you, honey. Sleep well."[4]

We settle for the counterfeit and less-than-His-best because it's within our reach. But God wants to bless us with the real thing—an answer that goes wide and deep, and affects how we live and parent, and how we look at marriage. We might have to content ourselves with waiting for it, but when He delivers the breakthrough, we are never the same.

God is speaking and pouring Himself out to a waiting and watching world. The problem is, the majority are neither waiting nor watching. Oh, may we feast on the best and healthiest of what God has for us, and not merely grab for the candy that's at hand. There's a world out there in need of the fresh life to which we have access.[5]

SPIRITUAL LIFT:

"Waiting in the sunshine of His love is what will ripen the soul for His blessing. . . . Be assured that if God waits longer to answer than you anticipated, it is only to make the blessing all the more precious. . . . Our times are in His hands."

□ *Andrew Murray*[6]

You have a dream in your womb. You have a desire in your heart. Your answer is not in your husband, though you may feel otherwise. I challenge you to think on a deeper level: You're not waiting for your husband to come around spiritually, be more

□

available, or get well. You are waiting on the Lord God Almighty who means what He says when He says *He will come through for you.* (See Isaiah 30:18; 64:4.)

When we think of the "wait" as a useless weight that wastes our time, we miss out on one of the most precious parts of our journey. If in our waiting season, we fix our gaze straight ahead on our destination rather than on the journey itself, we will soon become rigid travelers who have lost the pleasure and wonder of the journey. Bored and rigid travelers leave fresh expectations behind in the dust.

As children of God, we must never lose the hopeful expectation that He is on the move and is busy and active in our lives. Waiting is not about biding our time, tapping our toe, or singing without a song. Waiting, when harnessed as an opportunity for God to show up, will become one of the sweetest burdens we will ever carry.

I would rather be walking hand in hand with Jesus while aching and waiting for my breakthrough, than to live in a house where everything goes my way, but the only sound I hear is the echo of my selfish soul. This psalmist felt the same way. "Better is one day in your courts than a thousand elsewhere; I would rather be a doorkeeper in the house of my God than dwell in the tents of the wicked" (Psalm 84:10 NIV).

But practically speaking, how do we hang on to hopeful expectation? How do we capture the waiting season that we might be renewed? Here are a few thoughts.

PLANT FLOWERS   Be good to you!

Let's start with the simple things. It's especially important amidst the waiting seasons that you treat yourself to little moments of joy. Make sure you "plant flowers" on your journey. Take time to do sweet things for yourself—light a candle and listen to music; get a pedicure and have lunch with a friend; buy yourself a fresh bouquet; read a book—and try your best not to carry your husband's burdens for him.

HAND HIM OVER *let God deal with your husband.*

It will take great discipline of thought and heart to leave your cares in the Lord's hands, but I know you can do it. "Praise be to the Lord, to God our Savior, who daily bears our burdens" (Psalm 68:19 NIV). Here is another version of this powerful verse: "Praise the Lord; praise God our savior! For each day he carries us in his arms" (NLT).

Entrust your husband to God. Entrust your *hopes for him* to God. Carrying God's portion of your husband's burden will crush you. Trust that God has heard you during this time of waiting. Trust that He is working in your husband's life too, and when you are tempted to take matters into your own hands, remind yourself that God is carrying your husband in His arms.

CHANGE YOUR POSTURE *Expect God to deliver!*

Change the way you approach God. Lean, wait, listen, expect. Don't compartmentalize your faith where in the morning you're doing your dutiful devotions and in the afternoon you've forgotten that you're actively—not a biding-your-time-passive wait but an active one—waiting on the Lord until the breakthrough comes. Live each day in a holy expectation. God is at work, and soon your eyes will see it.

May your whole being be unrelenting with your expectant waiting on God until your breakthrough comes! Posture yourself as a woman in waiting, and expect God to deliver on His promises. Not only will you see powerful answers to your faith-filled prayers; you will be renewed because you've spent so much time wrestling with and getting to know God.

Remember, too, that this waiting season is only training ground for a greater purpose. Whatever disappointments or frustrations you carry in your marriage or because of your husband, look above them. This isn't about your marriage or even your husband. This is about *you*, about your spiritual journey. What will you do with the journey to which you've been assigned?

And how will you handle that which God is *not* giving you right now? *Keep looking up!*

You have certain dreams in your soul: dreams for your family, dreams for your marriage, and dreams that reflect the gifts God has put inside of you. Will you live and breathe and pray as though you are about to give birth . . . or not? Will waiting drain you or renew you? *Renew me!*

Dear friend, lean into the One your soul loves, let your face glow as one who is expectant, and walk on in victory. Do not be passive in your waiting. Be eager.

"But we who live by the Spirit eagerly wait to receive by faith the righteousness God has promised to us" (Galatians 5:5).

LENDING A HAND

Watch Your Step—Be careful not to allow the waiting to get old. Plant flowers, talk to friends, and keep your hope and expectation alive. You are traveling toward a promise; put one foot in front of the other; keep your eyes on the prize, and walk on in faith.

Stay on the Right Path—Remember what the Word of God says about you, your husband, and your situation. Every day, picture yourself as a woman in waiting, expectant with a promise. Take care of your soul the way a pregnant woman cares for her body. Nourish yourself, rest in the Lord, and get excited about giving birth!

Run From—Run from the tendency to develop an attitude. Determine not to "hope in your husband." Run from the temptation of talking too much about how your husband is letting you down. This will make the journey seem long and God's promises seem too far out of reach.

Destination Ahead—Run toward friends who fuel your faith. Ask God for a fresh vision for your life. Ask Him to show you which promises are yours to claim in this season of life. Write these things down. Keep them ever before you. Spend much time with God, and posture yourself as a woman in waiting.

Watch the Fine Line—You will have moments of boredom in your prayers and frustration in your faith. But don't allow those moments to become days that can turn into weeks. Take those moments and declare, "By the authority of Christ Jesus, I put these things under my feet! I am a woman waiting for a promise and I will not be denied! No matter how I *feel* today, I will act and live and choose my perspective based on what the Word says! I receive by faith a fresh dose of joy and peace and perspective!"

God's Promise for You Today— "Since before time began no one has ever imagined, no ear heard, no eye seen, a God like you *who works for those who wait for him*" (Isaiah 64:4 THE MESSAGE).

Precious Bridegroom,

*You are all that I need. Help me, Lord, to lean in and listen. I
will rest in the shadow of Your wings because You are my help,
and You will establish Your purposes for me. Come, and break
through in my life. Break through the sameness and bring a
fresh, new breeze of Your Spirit. Take the yoke that I carry
and put a new spring in my step. Teach me how to turn my
waiting season into a time of deep renewal and hopeful
expectation. My soul waits on You, Lord. Amen.*

Amen

TO THINK ABOUT...

1. Read Habakkuk 2:1–3

a. Let's start with the first part of verse 1. There are two
components to his posture: to stand and to look. As you
have walked through this season waiting for things to
change, how have you taken your stand and looked for
the Lord specifically in regard to your marriage? Explain.

b. Is this a once-in-a-while posturing, or do you
approach the Lord on a regular basis, take up the active
stance of waiting, and then look to see what the Lord has
to say? Describe if or how you "actively wait" for the
Lord to bring a breakthrough in your marriage.

2. Read verses 2–3 again

a. Looking at verse 2, spend a moment in prayer; ask
God to give you a godly vision for your marriage. What
does it look like? Where do you want to be in five years?

How will your finances, lovemaking, date nights, time management, and child rearing be affected if God has His way? Write down a vision and make it plain!

b. Did the "vision exercise" give you hope or make you feel hopeless? Explain.

c. As you prayerfully read verse 3, what do you sense God is saying to you? Write it down.

3. Read Isaiah 64:3–4

a. Write a personalized prayer from this passage.

b. Time for listening prayer. I want you to use Isaiah 40:28–31 as your guideline. God is the Creator of heaven and earth, and He greatly blesses those who wait for Him.

4. This exercise will take you about five minutes (although feel free to take longer!). Find a quiet spot: put on some instrumental or worshipful music. Get comfortable and rest in the Lord. Don't check out mentally; put your thoughts on the Lord. Imagine Him pouring strength into you; use this time to nourish your soul. Record your thoughts afterward.

QUALIFIED FOR THE CLIMB

MY FRIENDS live in a gated community up near the top of a mountain. I often stay with them for a few days when I am in town for a writers' conference. One day I decided to hike down and then up the mountain again.

My friends asked, "Are you sure you want to hike this mountain? We have another friend who tried the hike; she is an avid runner and yet needed to be picked up at the halfway mark."

I looked out the window at the beautiful day and smiled. "If it takes me all day, I'll make it back up this mountain!"

It was a sharp descent and a very hot day. Once I got to the bottom of the mountain, I stretched a little and drank about half of the water in my bottle.

Putting one foot in front of the other, I began the climb. I leaned into the hill and mostly walked on the balls of my feet. The air was thick and the climb was steep. At one point I looked up and what I saw took my breath away. The mountain was huge. Trees stretched to the heavens; rocky cliffs jutted out at severe angles. The road bent right then left and then wound out of sight.

As I stood there with my eyes gazing upward, I realized that I was no match for this mountain. Its very size overwhelmed me.

Just then I heard a very distinct whisper across my heart: *"Remember this."* I looked up at the majesty of God's handiwork and I was thoroughly intimidated. Not because I was tired, but because I was small next to this very large mountain.

I put my feet to work and with one step in front of the other, I moved upward. I climbed and sang and prayed, and though my breathing rate increased, I thoroughly enjoyed myself.

I thought I was only halfway up the hill when I saw the turn for my friends' house. I thought I had much farther to climb; though I was covered in sweat, I was not overcome by exhaustion. Again I heard the whisper: *"Remember this."*

I knew this story was for you and me.

Whatever mountains stand in your way, when your way seems too steep to climb, *remember this*: With the Lord on your side, you have what it takes. You've been conditioned and prepared for such a time as this. You can't conquer the mountain all at once, but with God at your side, you can put that thing under your feet one step at a time.

In this third and final section of the book, we will explore what qualifies us to take on the mountains that stand in our way.

SECTION THREE

□

We are valuable and we are vessels of the Most High God. We are in a unique position to affect the lives of our husbands, our children, and our world. Understanding the *weight* of *our* perspective, *our* words, *our* prayers, and *our* faith-hope-and-love, will keep us climbing ever higher and reaching for the best of what God has for us.

You've come this far. Check the straps on your bag of wisdom and join me for the rest of the journey.

Nine

PERSPECTIVE

*I see the limits to everything human, but the
horizons can't contain your commands!*

*Oh, how I love all you've revealed;
I reverently ponder it all the day long.*

Psalm 119:96–97 THE MESSAGE

I SAT ON the beach with my teenage friend, totally engaged in what she had to say. With her knees to her chest, her hands holding her toes, and her eyes looking out over the water, she shared her story with me.

My friend lived in a tiny home and ate one slightly decent meal a day. Her sister relentlessly taunted her and treated her like a second-class citizen. When she didn't know the answer to a math problem at school, some of the boys told her that she was a waste of sperm. She had been sexually abused by a man in her neighborhood.

One night in a heated rage her sister tore through her bedroom and turned everything upside down, literally. My little friend fought back, and in a matter of minutes, the two were in an all-out brawl.

□

Scratched and bruised, and totally ashamed, she ran from her home and found a place to hide on the very beach where we were sitting. After the fight with her sister, she crawled underneath an overturned boat and spent the night. All night long gnats feasted on her cuts and scratches.

My mouth hung open as I listened to this beautiful, young girl tell such a wretchedly painful story. And just as I was about to wrap my arms around her, she turned and looked at me with a sparkle in her eye and a smile on her face.

She said something I will never forget. "Though life has bruised and beaten me, and Satan would love for me to think I am nothing and my situation is hopeless, *this is not what the Lord Jesus says of me*! I know He loves me, I know He has plans for my life, and nothing will keep me from His plans. I want to be like Oprah and accomplish big things, and then help poor girls like me. I am not made to live like this."

Even though most boys and men have treated her with contempt, my friend is quite positive that God is preparing a godly, kind, and caring husband just for her. She wants to be a wife and a mother, and she wants to help many girls just like her. There's no doubt in my mind that she will.

Now that's perspective.

My friend is a living, breathing expression of Psalm 73:23–24, which is a call to perspective and a call to hope. Dear friend, I ask you to do the same. List all of the reasons why you should not have a renewed perspective. List every circumstance that threatens your joy. Then tag this verse to the end of your list: "*Yet*, I still belong to you. You hold my right hand. You guide me with your counsel, leading me to a glorious destiny!"

Your circumstances are true. But truer still is the "yet" in this verse. No matter what earthly battles we endure or mountains we face, nothing can change the fact that we belong to the Most High God. One who is high above our circumstances. One who sees further than we can imagine. One who redeems every lost thing in our lives.

We have every reason to echo my friend and say, "Though life has bruised and beaten me, and Satan would love for me to think I am nothing and my situation is hopeless, *this is not what the Lord Jesus says of me*! I know He loves me, I know He has plans for my life, and nothing will keep me from His plans."

What's in your view today? If a close friend walked up to you and asked, "What's on your mind?" what would you say? Do things look bleak and hopeless? Or maybe they're not that extreme. Maybe things just seem old and redundant with no sign of change. Or perhaps it's finances that make your eyes blur and leave a pit in your stomach. During our one-sided season, I got discouraged every time I looked around the house at all of the projects that were half done.

Do you need a fresh perspective today? Look around you; survey your circumstances. Where do you see flowers growing or hear kind words or spot acts of kindness? In other words, where do you see God moving? Is it in your children? Go kneel down beside them and pray for them. Ask for a renewed perspective and a fresh wind of faith to blow through your home.

God is moving somewhere in your life. Find Him. Listen to what He has to say. Do what He says. Obey Him quickly. Ask the Lord to lift you up and show you your circumstances from *His* perspective. Ask to see your husband through His eyes. Then move forward, do what He tells you, and determine not to live a life of unbelief.

Don't worry about missing it. If there is *anything* in us that longs for God's highest plan for our lives, if there's anything in us that is bent toward obeying His voice, He will be found by us. He will get His answer to us. It's the prideful, rebellious heart that misses God. But the one with the humble, earnest heart—she will find Him and meet Him in the most unexpected places.

This is how we find the highest ground. We look around and look for God. When we find Him, we sit with Him for a while. We ask Him to tell us a few stories, sing us a few songs, and teach us how to climb.

Jesus longs for us to turn to Him. He is waiting to show us a better way to look at things. But to see Him, we have to look up. "Don't shuffle along, eyes to the ground, absorbed with the things right in front of you. Look up, and be alert to what is going on around Christ—that's where the action is. See things from *his* perspective" (Colossians 3:2 THE MESSAGE).

Not that we ignore the low places in our lives or pretend they don't exist. But we lose sight of the victory that awaits us if our eyes see only defeat. In the next three chapters we will talk about how to walk into those low places and find the promises of God so that no rock will be unturned.

First, we're talking about a godly perspective. Today we learn about the importance of climbing to the high spots and getting a panoramic view of the places to which we are traveling. High above what our eyes see is a God who is answering our prayers and making a difference in our marriages. Though our husbands may *look* the same and we may *feel* no different, God is at work on our behalf.

☐

Being reminded of that next place of promise fuels us to keep going. Having the assurance that God has something better for us keeps us learning, growing, and living. Tired as we may be at times, we were made for the climb. And no mountain stands a chance with Jesus at our side. He is the King of the mountains!

Here's a great story that illustrates how the mountains refine us and how God provides for us along the way:

Two months after our second child was born, my husband, Rob, received orders to report to his next navy job assignment aboard a ship that was stationed three hours away. We would have to sell the house, move again, and leave the home and friends we loved. As if that was not bad enough, we soon learned that the ship and its crew were preparing to leave for a six-month overseas deployment. The timing could not be worse. I already felt overwhelmed with the postpartum blues, a two-and-a-half-year-old toddler, and a newborn baby.

The day Rob had to report for his new assignment came and went without a serious offer from a prospective home buyer. The children and I stayed as he left for his new job. The impending six-month deployment drew closer as my fears escalated. I felt completely unprepared and unequipped to run a household without the support of my husband.

Deployment day came and the house was still for sale. I was completely overwhelmed by the responsibilities I faced. I began to seek the Lord like never before. Through days of intense prayer and seeking God's face, I came to understand more fully His loving provision for our lives. I took time to seek direction from His Word. I learned to cling to one treasured passage in particular—Proverbs 3:5–6. The passage states: "Trust in the

□

Lord with all your heart and lean not on your own understanding; in all your ways acknowledge him, and he will make your paths straight."

This passage was extremely helpful in my daily surrender to His will. When the washing machine or car broke down or when the children were sick—I trusted Him and He saw me through each day.

I began to realize like never before how much God cared for me as an individual. His truth helped me to grow the confidence in my abilities to take care of my family. By the end of the six-month deployment, my fears had been relinquished, while my skills, abilities, and confidence grew. Most important, my relationship with God grew closer than it had ever been.

—Valerie from Michigan

We are the ones who have to put feet to our faith. He has provided everything we need for overwhelming victory. He has equipped us to conquer all of the high and low places. He has equipped us, but *we* need to walk it out. So how do we lose perspective, and how do we gain it?

HOW TO LOSE ALTITUDE
Forgetfulness—unbelief—grumbling

"You saw what he did in the wilderness, how God, your God, carried you as a father carries his child, carried you the whole way until you arrived here. But now that you're here, you won't trust God, your God—this same God who goes ahead of you in your travels to scout out a place to pitch camp, a fire by night and a cloud by day to show you the way to go. When God heard (your complaining), he exploded in anger. He swore, 'Not a single person of this evil generation is going to get so much as a look at the good land that I promised to give to your parents. Not one'" (Deuteronomy 1:31–35 THE MESSAGE).

It's all too easy to lose sight of who we are and what we are called to, but we must not. Even when we simply feel like wives who are overlooked, overworked, and in need of a good haircut, even then we are representatives of the Most High God.

God has done great things for us in the past. He is faithful in our present. Though we may have hardships in our marriage, we are still called to belief, still called to remember, and still called to perspective. We have everything we need for our climb. We have in our hands a recipe for victory.

There is a big difference between pouring our heart out to God or to God-fearing friends, and complaining. Complaining looks down, forgets all God has done, and cultivates an unbelieving heart. Complaining adds a heavy weight to your load. And here's a good way to add so much weight that the straps on your bag are strained to the point of breaking—join with other women and complain about your husbands!

Jesus' yoke for us is easy and His burden is light. He acknowledges there would be *many* trials and sorrows in this life. But in the same sentence He calls us to a godly perspective. He tells us to take courage, to be of good cheer, because He, after all, has overcome the world! (See John 16:33.)

Marriage can be hard work and a steep climb. Some of our husband's actions will cause us to lose perspective and even our footing.

If our husband is too busy to pay the phone bill and our phone is turned off, we may have to battle to remember that his choices don't define us. If he makes a business decision that drains the savings account, we may have to look more earnestly to the Lord and gain a deeper reliance on *Him*. If our husband chooses a time-consuming hobby and refuses to see its impact on the family, along with using tough love and firm communication, we may work to curb an attitude that will seek to get away from us.

We may trip over their words and have to grab hold of the Word to get back to a place of peace. God will occasionally use our husband's earthbound nature to challenge us to reach for a higher perspective.

Even though our husband's humanity will weigh heavily upon us at times, God is serious when He says that He hates complaining. I'm sure our grumbling words sound like nails on a chalkboard to Him.[1]

I remember a specific time when God spoke to my heart about complaining. I had made a sincere commitment to pay close attention to what comes out of my mouth. One day when I was particularly frustrated about something, I was tempted to complain but remembered my commitment to the Lord. I kept my mouth shut until I got into my car. I was driving somewhere and I figured it might be safe to vent with no one listening (uh, no one, that is, except God). As soon as I got into my car, I heard the whisper across my heart, *"Don't do it."*

So I began praising instead. I thanked God out loud for everything good around me. I thanked Him for the presence of the Holy Spirit in my life, who guides me every minute of the day. Literally, in a matter of moments, my spirit was buoyed up and I was overjoyed with a perspective that was *above* my circumstances.

This experience created a picture in my mind of riding in a beautiful hot-air balloon. I could look down and see the vast horizon and landscape. My problem was *on the ground*; it was small and out of sight because I was overcome by the greater creation of my intimate and personal God.

When I open my mouth and allow words of complaint and grumbling to escape, I lose altitude. My balloon drops along with my perspective. Let this be a picture for you too. Refuse a grumbling spirit. Hold yourself in high regard before the Lord. Don't forget all of the ways He has come through for you. Refuse to let go of the fact that He has gone ahead and is working on your behalf. Embrace the truth that He walks beside you with His hand of blessing on your head.[2]

"In everything you do, stay away from complaining and arguing" (Philippians 2:14 NLT).

HOW TO GAIN ALTITUDE
Think clearly—look forward—be holy

"So think clearly and exercise self-control. Look forward to the gracious salvation that will come to you when Jesus Christ is revealed to the world. So you must live as God's obedient children. Don't slip back into your old ways of living to satisfy your own desires. You didn't know any better then. But now you must be holy in everything you do, just as God who chose you is holy. For the Scriptures say, 'You must be holy because I am holy'" (1 Peter 1:13–16).

We've already talked a bit about our thought life, but a few more words are merited here. Our thinking has everything to do with our perspective! We will never scale the heights and see with eyes of faith without renewing our minds. Though it will take great effort to line up our thoughts and make them consistent with God's Word, this is a good fight, and one we must practice daily if we want our lives to be continually transformed and our eyes to see new horizons.

I remember a time when I was getting ready to leave for a speaking engagement. I woke up to a grey, cloudy day. The heaviness of the weather greatly affected my mood and energy level. But once I got on the plane and we took off, I saw something that would forever change the way I think and pray.

The plane climbed higher and higher. We flew into the clouds and then above the clouds. Once we put the clouds under us, we were flying in a bright blue sky! It was a beautiful day above the clouds! I determined from that point on that I would never allow the clouds (literal or figurative) to oppress me for very long. Whatever it takes, I pray, I seek, and I think thoughts of praise until I get on the other side of those heavy moments, because it's always a beautiful day when you're above the clouds.

At first, thinking clearly requires a moment-by-moment application. Eventually, after you've immersed your thoughts in what is true and right and good, it becomes almost instinctive to think in ways that lift you up. Not to say our thoughts don't require our regular attention; they do. But your life will be transformed and horizons will appear when you regularly renew your perspective. "Fix your thoughts on what is true and honorable and right. Think about things that are pure and lovely and admirable. Think about things that are excellent and worthy of praise. Keep putting into practice all you learned from me and heard from me and saw me doing, and the God of peace will be with you" (Philippians 4:8–9 NLT).

Regarding the call to look forward, I have a good friend who shared a piece of wisdom I want to pass along to you. We were at a wedding shower the other day, and my friend Judy said this:

P E R S P E C T I V E

"During my tougher seasons in marriage, most of my friends were in the same boat as I was. They were my age, and we were all struggling in the same way.

"It wasn't until I befriended a few godly women who were older and wiser than I, that I gained perspective. They'd already been down my road, and were much further along in their walk of faith. They were able to call me higher, and I was able to respond to what they had to say. For me, perspective happened when I allowed myself to learn from those who had already gone before me."

Part of looking forward is calling out to those who are further up the mountain and asking them, "What do you see? Tell me, does it get easier? How has God come through for you? What have you learned?"

Look forward by humbling yourself and learning from those ahead of you. Look forward by looking up to a God who will faithfully come through for you. Look forward by looking out and surveying the next place of promise that is yours for the taking. With one foot in front of the other, keep moving.

When you respond to the call to climb this mountain when other mountains look more attractive, engaging, or easier to climb—and you do so with humility, love, obedience, and hope—you are made holy as you go.

Anyone can *seem* holy alone in a cabin up in the mountains away from anything that is living and breathing. But to walk along with imperfect people who personally affect your life, and to love them when it is easier not to, is to follow in Christ's footsteps.

Perspective happens when we see things from God's point of view, and then we choose to live by following the footsteps of His Son.

SPIRITUAL LIFT:

"The whole outlook of mankind might be changed if we could all believe that we dwell under a friendly sky and that the God of heaven, though exalted in power and majesty, is eager to be friends with us."

A. W. Tozer[3]

There are limits to what our earthly eyes can see, but the horizons cannot contain the awesomeness of God! Lift up your heads. Look up! Dare not to walk through this earth as a bruised beggar, when you are armed with heaven on your side!

LENDING A HAND

Watch Your Step—Be careful not to allow your circumstances to define your perspective. Every day, take a moment to climb to the high ground and ask for a renewed perspective. Allow your thoughts to be consumed with God's love for you, His faithfulness to you, and His promise to lead you through to victory.

Stay on the Right Path—Remember who you are. You are a representative of the Most High God, regardless of how you feel today. Others are counting on your perspective. In fact, how you look at things will affect what choices you make; and your choices will create a ripple effect that will last long after you are gone from this earth. Choose a higher perspective.

Run From—Run from grumbling, complaining, unbelief, and conversations that weigh you down. Avoid these things like the plague. Though the path gets rough, it's still holy ground. Walk and climb with God on your mind.

Destination Ahead—Run toward godly women who have been where you are. Pursue a heart of gratitude and praise. Be buoyed up by words of thanks. Run after a renewed mind-set. Hold tightly to your commitment to obey even when your eyes can't see.

Watch the Fine Line—Even when the mountain is so huge that it hurts your neck to look at it, you are called to belief. Refuse to be intimidated by the obstacles that stand in your way! But always know that you're no match for them without the presence of the Lord in your midst. Follow where He leads. Rest when He tells you to. Admit your need, but believe for great things.

God's Promise for You Today—"I ask—ask the God of our Master, Jesus Christ, the God of glory—to make you intelligent and discerning in knowing him personally, your eyes focused and clear, so that you can see exactly what it is he is calling you to do, grasp the immensity of this glorious way of life he has for his followers, oh, the utter extravagance of his work in us who trust him—endless energy, boundless strength! All this energy issues from Christ: God raised him from death and set him on a throne in deep heaven" (Ephesians 1:17–20 THE MESSAGE).

Father,

I ask for heaven's perspective today. Draw me close, lift up my head, and open my eyes to see the wonder of Your love. Help me to slow down long enough to listen to the birds sing and appreciate the ever-changing sky. May these evidences of Your handiwork inspire me to believe. I will rejoice because You care for me. Inspire me, Lord, for this climb. Fill me up with love for my husband, and give me a heart for this mountain. Meet me here and show me the horizons. Give me a picture of my Promised Land. Grant me strength to keep climbing. I only want to be with You. Amen.

TO THINK ABOUT...

1. Read Colossians 3:1–2

a. Describe what it means to you to be raised with Christ. How does this truth directly affect *your* circumstances? Explain.

b. We've been offered every spiritual blessing we need to live a life of wholeness (see Ephesians 1:3), and yet in order to possess all that's been offered, steps need to be taken by us. Verse 1 tells us to take one such step. What is it, and how are you currently applying this challenge in your own life?

c. Verse 2 gives another clear directive. How is this different than the charge in verse 1? Again, how do you carry this out in your own life?

☐

2. Read Habakkuk 3:17–19

a. Rewrite verse 17 in your own words (e.g., *Though my savings account is empty and my body is tired, and though . . .*), and then tag on verse 18 to the end of your paraphrased prayer. You are becoming a powerful prayer warrior!

b. When battling for perspective, which of the things mentioned in your prayer challenges your perspective the most? Explain.

c. Look at verse 19 again. Who is your strength and what will He enable you to do? Write it down. Will you take His hand and let Him lead you to those higher places and perspectives in regard to your marriage? Write a prayer telling Him so.

3. Read Psalm 18:28–36

a. I absolutely love this passage! I believe God has something very special for you in this Scripture. Pick a portion of this passage that most speaks to you and write it out in a declarative, personalized prayer. Declare that your victory and strength comes from the Lord, because it does! Your perspective comes from Him!

b. Let's stay with the Psalm 18 passage for another moment. Pick a portion of this passage and use it as a guideline for your listening prayer exercise. Enjoy!

4. This exercise requires that you step off the beaten path for a moment or two. Find a high point somewhere around where you work or live. You may have to go to one of the top floors of a high-rise and look out the window or drive somewhere and climb to the top of a hill. Personally, I would rather you fully engage in this exercise by climbing a hill. Feel the strain in your legs and the challenge to your lungs. Once you get to the top of your hill, look all around you. Appreciate the view and embrace the higher perspective. *Remember this.*

Ten

GOD'S WORDS

MOUNTAINS MOVE
WHEN YOU SPEAK GOD'S WORDS

Then Jesus said to the disciples, "Have faith in God.
I assure you that you can say to this mountain, 'May
God lift you up and throw you into the sea,' and your
command will be obeyed. All that's required is
that you really believe and do not doubt in your heart."

□ Mark 11:22–23 NLT

I'D LIKE TO tell you another story about the time I was in Belize, because nowhere else have I experienced such a tangible battle between the demonic forces of hell and the forces of heaven— and the power available to those who belong to Jesus. I wrote this in my journal while I was there: "I am in a place where I am quite sure that every single day angels and demons pass each other by on the street."

We were in a small, poverty-stricken village where dogs run wild and are often abused. These animals had a crazed look in their eyes and responded to the demonic activity level in the village by barking ferociously.

One day three of my friends and I were walking to the church. We turned onto a road we had taken many times before, but for some reason this time everything felt different.

There were no moms out and about doing their everyday chores, and no children around playing. Instead there were several groups of scary men who looked like they were stoned, glaring at us with scowling eyes. Music was playing, drums were beating in the background, and dogs running in packs were all around, barking at us at a feverish pitch. We felt such a thick darkness pressing in and enveloping us that we could almost cut it with a knife. Suddenly we were outnumbered and felt isolated.

A couple of men narrowed their eyes and stepped toward us. They were saying things in their native language. By the tone of their voices and the expressions on their faces I knew they weren't telling us to "Have a nice day." My friend Ann grabbed my hand and I began to sing, "Jesus, what a wonder You are; You are so gentle, so pure and so kind; You shine like the morning star; Jesus, what a wonder You are."[1] Ann began to harmonize with me. We looked straight ahead, singing, walking, and refusing to be intimidated by the oppression around us.

Instantly, the presence of darkness was pushed back, making room for us to walk down an alleyway of light and peace. The dogs and the men stepped back a bit and continued to make noise, but their impact faded into the background. We kept singing and kept walking.

Ann later described our worshipful prayer as a sword of light cutting through the darkness. For me, it was one of the most tangible expressions of God's power making a way through the darkness that I have ever experienced.

⁂

Maybe we all know this, but it's good to be reminded who our Enemy really is—and it's *not* our husbands! "For we are not fighting against flesh-and-blood enemies, but against evil rulers and authorities of the unseen world, against mighty powers in this dark world, and against evil spirits in the heavenly places" (Ephesians 6:12).

When the road gets rough and the climb gets steep, the lines get blurred; and it's easy to lose sight of whom or what it is we're fighting. Imagine if you will, you and your husband backpacking and hiking in the mountains, glowing with sweat and covered in bug bites. You're in a difficult part of the climb. Suddenly you see a mountain lion coming toward you, licking his chops.

Just as the lion is readying himself to pounce, you recall how your husband made *you* tear down the tent this morning just so *he* could take a dip in the lake.

You're suddenly so furious that you jump on your husband's back and begin calling him names. "Idiot! Selfish! Stupid!" You claw at him with your fingernails and kick him with your thick hiking boots. You're on your husband's back with your arms around his face and your feet wrapped around his waist pounding on his back when, out of the corner of your eye, you see the lion quietly slip back into the bushes and go away.

Now as ridiculous as this sounds, the Bible does say that the Devil roams around like a lion, looking for someone whom *he may devour*. But the lion is especially satisfied if he can get Christians to do his dirty work for him.

How do we devour our husbands, you ask? We are on their backs and in their faces. We nag, we roll our eyes, and at times we even say terrible things about them to our friends. We devour them by the things we do and the things we don't do. We withhold compliments, respect, and affectionate touch when it's within our means to do these things. In fact, nobody can (or is supposed to) fill the needs of his life like we can.

We sometimes say and do things that are spiteful and non-supportive when our husbands act like the sinners they are. The Bible says that life and death are in our words and that a whole city can either be established or destroyed by our words. We are called to bless those who curse us, love those who act hateful toward us, and give to those who are already taking from us. [2]

Never mind if the recipient is "deserving" of our verbal bullets; do we really want to be an accomplice to the Enemy's work? We will be deeply hurt at times, and our natural response is to lash out in terrible ways. In fact, we have all no doubt already struck back in ways that should have been beneath us. We've all had to ask forgiveness for the things we've said. It's never been about what others deserve—it's always been about what response God deserves from us.

These are tough words to write and even tougher words to read, because I know your situation might be one where doing the lion's work sounds like just what is called for. But if we can step back a bit and bring ourselves before the Lord, we can remember that *He loves us all*; even when we're hateful. And the Enemy hates us all, especially when we walk in love like Jesus did.

The Enemy comes to steal what's ours, kill the fresh life that God is birthing in us, and destroy our hopes for an abundant, fruitful future. He is the one who is at work trying to tear us apart, hoping we'll turn on each other. He is our Enemy and he puts mountains in our paths, hoping we will breathe a heavy sigh and resign ourselves to remaining forever down in the valleys.

He is hoping against hope that we will not believe Jesus when He tells us that we can simply speak to our mountains in faith and they will move; because if our words begin to line up with God's, those mountains don't stand a chance.

The Devil knows the incredible power God has placed on our words. The question is, Do we know it? Do we really know that every time we open our mouths we affect the spiritual climate around us? God has entrusted us with such a gift, that unless we begin to believe Him, we will do more harm than good with our words.

The Bible says that life and death are in the tongue, and that we will have to eat the "fruit of our lips" (see Proverbs 18:21).

Whenever you speak, imagine little seeds spilling out of your mouth and sinking into the soil in the ground. Those seeds bear fruit; sometimes good fruit, sometimes not. What you sow, you will grow. It's both our privilege and our responsibility to watch our words, to bless others with our words, and to praise God with our words.

This worked for me: Ask God for a heightened sensitivity to His Spirit regarding the things you say. Ask for extra grace to be protected during your weak and vulnerable moments. Ask for courage to walk away from toxic conversations. And ask to be interrupted before you have a chance to say something you'll later regret.

SPIRITUAL LIFT:

"No matter what the Enemy tries to tell you, Christ is God of the mountains and God of the valleys."

Francis Frangipane[3]

NAME YOUR MOUNTAIN!
Is it your husband? Then declare,

- □ By faith, I proclaim that my husband is doing his best to present himself to God as one approved, a workman who does not need to be ashamed and who correctly handles the word of truth (see 2 Timothy 2:15).

- □ God is helping him to be very careful about how he lives, with great wisdom and discernment (see Ephesians 5:15–16).

- □ In Jesus' name, I proclaim that he will not be led into temptation; he will be delivered from evil (see Matthew 6:13).

- □ By faith, I believe that God is giving him a love for me that is divine and supernatural. May he love me the way Christ loves His bride, the church (see Ephesians 5:25).

- □ With the authority I have in Christ, I release a blessing over his life! I declare that a revival of faith will soon begin in his heart (see Matthew 8:10)!

Is it that you don't feel loved? Then declare,

- □ I am my Beloved's and He is mine. His banner over me is love (see Song of Songs 2:4).

- □ God treasures me and loves me with an everlasting love (see Jeremiah 31:3).

□ My expectation is in God and I will not be disappointed. For I choose to know and believe that God dearly loves me. I believe it because He has given me His Holy Spirit to fill and overflow my heart with His love (see Romans 5:5).

□ Regardless of my imperfections and foibles, I can stand up and gratefully say that there is no condemnation for me, because I belong to Jesus! Oh, how You love me, Lord (see Romans 8:1).

□ I choose to trust in God's unfailing love, which is available to me daily. I will rejoice because He has rescued me before, and He'll rescue me again (see Psalm 13:5).

Is it fatigue and discouragement? Then declare,

□ I will bring my burden to the Lord and leave it there. I am promised that if I wait on the Lord, I will find new strength. I will fly high on wings like eagles'. I will run and not grow weary. I will walk and not faint. I know this kind of renewal is mine for the taking and I receive it in Jesus' name (see Isaiah 40:31).

□ I refuse a downcast spirit and I will put my hope in God (see Psalm 43:5).

God promised to refresh me when I am weary and satisfy my heart. I will wait for God to deliver on His promises (see Jeremiah 31:25).

171

□

Maybe your alone season in marriage is causing money worries, or has been caused by money problems. Is your mountain finances? Then declare,

- □ "My God shall supply all (our) needs according to His riches in glory in Christ Jesus!" (Philippians 4:19 HCSB)

- □ May our homes be bursting with blessings of every kind! May our accounts, investments, and even relationships flourish in the presence of the Lord! May there be no breached walls, no forced exile, and no cries of distress in our streets. Yes, happy are those who have it like this! Happy indeed are those whose God is the Lord (see Psalm 144:13–15).

- □ Soon we will be debt-free and our only debt will be to love one another (see Romans 13:8).

Your children play such a vital role in your own life and in your marriage. Is one of your mountains your children? Then declare,

- □ "May our sons flourish in their youth like well-nurtured plants. May our daughters be like graceful pillars, carved to beautify a palace" (Psalm 144:12–13).

- □ Our children are not rebellious. They know their spiritual heritage; they know they belong to the Lord and are therefore quick to honor and obey and their lives are blessed as a result (see Ephesians 6:1–3).

☐ Like Jesus, our children are growing in wisdom and stature and are loved by all who know them (see Luke 2:52).

☐ Even in stressful times, our children do not fear; they live and breathe and function with a spirit of power, love, and sound mind (see 2 Timothy 1:7).

Mountains condition us for the climb; they strengthen us for the battle, and they fuel us to claim what is rightfully ours because we belong to the Most High God. When we camp on the wrong side of the mountain and we use our words to bear witness against what God says is true, we are by our unbelief being insubordinate to our King.

The Bible says that day and night Jesus intercedes on our behalf (He does this for our husbands too), and day and night the Devil accuses us (and our husbands), finds fault with us (and our husbands), and picks apart every little thing we do. (Imagine the clash of kingdoms when those two streams of words meet in the heavenly places!)

If you've ever read Frank Peretti's *This Present Darkness*, you might have an easier time imagining this kind of scene.

Though we can't see them, the Bible tells us that we have warring angels who battle on our behalf. They are battling for truth, and they want us to fight for it too. The Bible also describes demons who daily steal, kill, destroy, deceive, and wage war against anyone in their paths. Their greatest goal is to get us to believe a lie. And since life and death are in the power of the tongue, there is a very real war being waged over what we believe, and thus, what we say.

Imagine that battle going on right over our heads. Now imagine a freeze-frame moment when all of the angelic and demonic forces look down and hold their breath because they see us opening our mouths, preparing to speak.

What springs forth from our lips? Are we in agreement with hell's voice over our lives? Do we repeatedly say things like this? "Things will never work out for me! We will never get this debt paid off. My husband will never change. I'm stuck with a rotten marriage. There is no hope for me." Or do we push back the Enemy forces with words of faith and belief, words in agreement with heaven's voice?

The powerful woman proclaims, "I don't see how this is going to work out, but thank the Lord, my times are in God's hands. My God will strengthen me and make all things new again. When my husband fails me and even breaks my heart, I will be reminded of the countless ways I fail the Lord with my own imperfections. I will forgive my husband as I've been forgiven. I will trust God to fill the places where my husband is lacking. I expect God to come through for me, and I refuse to relinquish in unbelief what God has promised me. God will be pleased by my faith in Him!"

You have things to say to your children about this bumpy season in your marriage. For whatever reason, their father isn't as available as he once was. The strain you are feeling is most likely obvious to your loved ones. You have things to say to your friends and your family about what you are experiencing.

Embarrassing . . . frustrating . . . wearying . . . and did I say embarrassing? Yes, that's how it felt to look like a single parent at school events, and so many other functions that were important to our children. I found myself consciously playing with my wedding ring, to draw attention to the fact that I really did have a husband.

It wasn't supposed to be like that. No one ever signs on for a marriage where they're going to have to carry most of the weight. Especially with sons. But those were the sacrifices of marriage to a husband who often traveled three weeks out of every month, tending to other flocks and sharing the gospel.

There were days of real despair. Sometimes there was anger and frustration when the children would ask, "Is Dad going to be able to make it to this meeting? You know it's really important!" For my husband and me, there were many debates about whether the ministry had a right to demand so much— and even more about whether he had a right to give so much. It seemed as though his priorities were confused. How could God expect him to give so much to the church and so little to his own family?

I refused to feel guilty about asking these questions. Because behind them was a deep longing to have a "normal" family. And there was an even greater longing to teach our children to love God and to love the work of God. Pastors' children have become notorious for straying from the church because it has taken their father from them. We so desperately wanted this to not happen to our family.

I made up my mind to never let the children see us arguing about the ministry. And to never complain about their father's absence. I always tried to encourage them to know how he was being used by God in such marvelous ways. And when he was home, he tried to make them as much of a priority as he could.

I'm sure we didn't do everything right. But by the grace of

God, today all four of them have a sincere love for God and for His work. Two of them followed their dad in the ministry. And one thing that I've noticed about all of them—especially our three sons—is a deliberate, sacrificial devotion to their children. I rejoice to see that for each of them, their families come first, and then the ministry. It's funny . . . sometimes as much can be learned from dysfunction as from health. God is gracious like that. And for that, I am eternally grateful.

—Karen from Chicago

How much to do you say to friends and family members? And what about the children? For each of these relationships, that boundary is a different one. Because each connection is different and complex in its own way, communicating about this situation presents its own unique challenge over and over again.

Depending on the ages and stages of your kids, you will have to determine the healthiest route to take. If your children are very young, you will obviously need to absorb the added stress of your one-sided season (sharing only with your closest friends) and keep the home as peaceful a place as possible. Adolescents will want to know more than they can handle, so discernment will have to be used at all times. They will want you to acknowledge that, yes, things are different. They may attempt to get you mad at your husband and may even instigate a debate about him. Though it may seem they are only interested in knowing the gory details and seeing the sparks fly, what's truer is that deep inside they want to know that things are still stable and that you are still honorable. If you have teens, you will find that they know (and understand) more than you think. Even with teens it differs on which ones will benefit from information and which ones will not. Pray for divine wisdom in this matter. Forgive yourself *when* you don't do it perfectly.

Then there are your family members, your friends, your acquaintances. I've known a number of strong, godly women who have walked through a one-sided time without too many people knowing. They leaned on God, they leaned on their close friends, but otherwise they held their words close and truly honored their husbands in doing so.

Not to say you have to nicely "package" your pain or that you should work hard to create an "all is well" appearance. But if we are honest, we can tend to overprocess things at times. And it's always better to be selective about what we say, and who we say it to.

You will need help along the way. You will need to admit it when things aren't going so well. But in all things, let faith be present in your words. Try your best to speak from a heart of faith, hope, and love. Whether talking to your mountain or about it, let Jesus' name be honored by the way you represent Him. Heaven knows about you. Hell knows about you. When you open your mouth, you set in motion a work that will either reinforce your bondage or contribute to your deliverance. "Those who love to talk will experience the consequences, for the tongue can kill or nourish life" (Proverbs 18:21 NLT).

LENDING A HAND

Watch Your Step—Be careful about getting caught up in "husband" conversations. Almost nothing good can come out of these times unless they are in the context of prayerful and godly support. Ask God to give you a heightened sensitivity to His Spirit before you speak. He wants to redeem your words! You will be surprised how He "slows down time," giving you the chance to choose your words wisely.

Stay on the Right Path—Remember to hide God's Word in your heart. Always have a verse that you are committing to memory. Take the time to ponder what that verse means to you and think of how you will live differently because of it. Plant the seed deep in your soul. Don't be satisfied with a surface sprout when your whole belief system can be altered by a word of truth. Be committed to your spiritual growth and be earnest about aligning your speech with God's.

Run From—Run from the tendency to talk too much. Silence can be golden. Ask the Lord if you should have a "phone fast" where you step back from friend conversations. Perhaps you can use that time for some "listening prayer." Rather than being the one who does the talking, allow God to tell you what is on His mind for you today.

Destination Ahead—Run toward women whose mouths are sanctified! If you meet a woman who walks in the fear of the Lord, invite her for coffee. Pick her brain. Ask her about her journey. Expect to have a younger woman knocking on your door someday and be ready for her.

Watch the Fine Line—To pursue speech that lines up with heaven is one of the most radical, life-altering things we can do. But this does not mean that we walk around denying the existence of pain, heartache, and struggle. Nothing is more irritating than talking with someone who refuses to allow conversations that involve the gut-wrenching questions in life. Jesus welcomes and can handle the tough questions, and we need people who will walk through these thorny places with us. May we all be able to discern when our words venture away from an honest pursuit of answer, to a quagmire of complaints and cynicism.

God's Promise for You Today—"God wants us to grow up, to know the whole truth and tell it in love—like Christ in everything. We take our lead from Christ, who is the source of everything we do. He keeps us in step with each other. His very breath and blood flow through us, nourishing us so that we will grow up healthy in God, robust in love (Ephesians 4:15–16 THE MESSAGE).

Precious Jesus,

Renew my words today! Forgive me for the countless ways my speech has dishonored You and the life You've given me. I long to be one who chooses words that line up with Your thoughts toward me. Give me a renewed passion for the Bible; give me an increased capacity to memorize and put into practice all that it says. Grant me faith-filled words that make Your kingdom principles a reality in my life. Move mountains in me; move mountains through me. In Jesus' name, I pray. Amen.

TO THINK ABOUT...

1. Read Proverbs 18:21

a. Describe a time when you could actually *feel* the power behind the words you were saying (good or bad).

b. Describe a time when you said something that seemed of little consequence to you but later you found had a big impact on someone else (good or bad).

c. If you have Jesus in your heart, you are a spiritual being. Your words carry a lot of weight. List some areas of your speech that need to be sanctified (e.g., anxious confessions, angry outbursts, gossip, fear-based comments, etc.). Write a prayer asking for God's help in this.

2. Read 1 Peter 3:8–12

a. To pursue harmony in the home and to return a blessing when insulted are not natural responses; they're *super*-natural. And to this you were called. The only way to walk in this kind of holiness is to walk closely with the One who is holy. Write a prayer asking God to draw you closely to His side; ask Him to breathe His words through your lips (see Isaiah 51:16).

b. Do you long to love life and see many good days? So do I! Look at verses 10 and 11. Write down the six things Scripture asks of us here, and for each, give a tangible, personal example of how you can walk this out in your life.

c. Look at verse 12. Do you see how attentive the Lord is to those who love Him? He's watching. He's listening. How does this make you feel? Explain.

3. Read Proverbs 12:14; Isaiah 50:4; and Isaiah 59:21

a. Our words have power, impact, and a ripple effect that goes on long after we are gone. Imagine knowing and believing that the words of our mouths reward us as surely as the work of our hands! If we really believed this, we would be speaking blessings over others and ourselves every minute of the day! Choose one or more of these verses and write a declarative (faith-filled) statement about the power and impact of your words (e.g., *Thank You, Lord, for giving me the Word, which sustains the weary. I know what to say and when to say it. . . .*)

b. Time for listening prayer. The Lord has something to say to you in regard to your words. He wants to pour blessings on you and through you. He doesn't want to run into a logjam of unbelief and negative confessions. Allow Him to speak to your heart.

4. This exercise requires a little extra effort. Find an accountability partner—someone whose walk with God you respect, someone who is more sanctified in her speech than you are. Tell her how much you want your words to be a wellspring of belief and blessing. Share your honest struggles. Give yourself permission to be human, but pursue the upward call.

Eleven

PRAYER

One day Jesus told his disciples a story to show them
that they should always pray and never give up.

Luke 18:1

WHEN I WAS four years old, I had a best friend named Bob. He was about a million years older than I was, but I didn't mind. He lived across the street, and without fail, he made time for me. It didn't matter if he was working in his garage or pulling weeds in his yard, when he saw me standing at the curb preparing to cross the street, he always smiled, stopped what he was doing, and watched for cars while I walked over to his house. I hung out with Bob quite often. In fact, I cringe when I think of how I treated his wife at times.

I remember sitting at Bob's table one day enjoying a nice visit, when his wife walked in the room. There I sat; my little four-year-old body slouched in a chair that was too big for me, looking up at my competition. I asked her to go make us some sandwiches. That wonderful saint smiled at me and returned a few moments later with a plate of sandwiches, milk, and cookies.

We eventually moved out of the neighborhood. When I was old enough, I would ride my bike over to Bob's house to make sure he was still alive and was still my friend. Each visit revealed a few more wrinkle lines, but that only made his smile sweeter. And each visit reminded me just what a precious woman he married. Something about their home made me feel especially secure.

Jump ahead about thirty years. I was attending the mayoral prayer breakfast for the city where I was raised. After twenty-seven years, my father was retiring from serving as the city's mayor.

It was a delightful breakfast and a powerful program. I was so proud when I heard my father speak. My husband and sons were sitting around the table with me, and I was especially moved by the heritage of faith represented there.

The breakfast ended and the crowd started to mingle. For whatever reason, I was the last one at my table. I looked at my watch and realized I had to quickly get out of there and get to my next appointment. I reached down to pick up my purse. The strap was stuck on the leg of the chair.

I bent over and began pulling up on the strap like someone trying to pull a giant weed out of the ground. I pulled and twisted, working to free my purse from the leg of the chair. Suddenly the purse strap broke, sending my elbows with full force into the stomach of a sweet older gentleman who was walking behind me.

He grabbed his stomach and tried to catch his breath. I apologized profusely and asked him if he was okay. I was afraid I damaged him permanently. I turned and asked for his forgiveness and he blurted out, "Susie?" I said, "Yes, I'm Susie. Do I know you?" He smiled brightly and stretched out his arms. "It's your friend Bob! I'm the janitor here! How are you doing, my dear?"

I wrapped my arms around him, and we had a wonderful time catching up. Toward the end of our conversation, he smiled and said, "I'm glad to know you're a woman of faith." I smiled wide and asked, "Bob, you know Jesus?" He warmly grabbed my hands and said, "My sweet wife and I have prayed for you often throughout the years. We were thrilled to know that you gave your life to Christ."

I was only four years old when we were friends and I didn't become a Christian until eighth grade. To find out that this dear man and his sweet (and patient) wife were influencing my life by their prayers completely overwhelmed me. My life changed because they were faithful in prayer.

⟞⟝

If I would have just lifted up the chair and unwound my strap like any normal, respectable person, I would never have "bumped into" Bob. What does this story have to do with alone times during one-sided seasons in marriage and prayers that change things? Well, I see several applications here but we'll talk about these two:

STABLE MARRIAGES HAVE AN IMPACT ON COMMUNITIES

Just today a good friend told me how a recent divorce has affected a certain neighborhood. The husband and wife live in separate houses and the children don't have friends over like they used to. Now the wife is living with her boyfriend, and the husband is so angry he is not stable. People have taken sides, kids have gotten overlooked in the shuffle, and a whole community is affected because of the breakdown of one couple.

I was only four years old when I hung out with Bob. And when I went over there for cookies and milk, I felt safe, I felt peace, and I knew that all was well. I had a good home life but to have another good home across the street made my four-year-old world an especially safe place to be.

When we work on our marriages and build love in our homes, we strengthen our neighborhoods. It matters that we have stable marriages and peaceful homes in our communities.

On an Easter afternoon with the ham baking in the oven and the table set for the coming celebration, my husband of over twenty years walked out the door and left. Because his angry departures and nonchalant returns had become frequent in the past two years, I assumed this day would be like all the others.

But it wasn't.

The ham finished baking, the table sat waiting, and the afternoon stretched into evening. When he didn't return, a numbness, a terrible dread settled over me. What if he didn't come back this time?

As days passed, I realized this wasn't a charade. He had really left me. The numbness gave way to fear, and the fear exploded within me like a hand grenade, tearing at my heart, scrambling my insides. How could he do this to me? How could he leave me? And how could God let it happen?

Weeks later, God broke through my fog of pain and got my attention through the words of a friend. "Don't let this get the best of you. Think about your kids and what's best for them. Focus on God and what He wants you to do."

Whenever fear gripped my heart during those next few days, my friend's words played over and over in my mind. God was using her to deliver a message to me, and I realized the peace that began to settle over me was the "peace that is beyond our understanding" spoken of in Philippians 4:7. For the first time I understood what it meant. His peace was indeed guarding my heart and mind.

As the months wore on, the separation from my husband took me through the darkest valleys. But each time my turbulent feelings grabbed hold to take me on an emotional roller coaster, I reached out to God to steady me. I taped Scriptures to the walls, journaled, listened to praise songs, and pored through the Bible.

It was a long, difficult journey, but God showed me I didn't have to make it alone. As I gave Him time to work in our lives, as I took my focus off my husband and focused on the Lord, God revealed to both my husband and me many things that grew us into the man and woman . . . and couple He wanted us to be. And when we restored our marriage three years later, God gave us a stronger marriage than before.

—Linda from central Florida

PRAYER HAS AN IMPACT ON THIS GENERATION AND THE NEXT

Marriage is worth fighting for, and prayer is the most effective way to battle for results. If only we had a glimpse of the activity taking place in heaven because of the prayers of God's people! Our lives are definitely better because someone before us labored in prayer. And consider that our lives could be more difficult and that we are exposed to an increased measure of evil in our day because some before us were too busy or didn't have the faith to pray.

We either give up or gain ground based on our faithfulness in prayer. Oh, may God give us eyes to see the impact of our intercession! When we live only in the moment, we lose sight of the bigger picture.

When we consider that God will be tending to our prayers long after we are gone, and that the world will either be blessed because we prayed or cursed because we didn't, we will be more stimulated to pray. When our families live in freedom and in peace and determine to walk in faith and love, we have created a ripple effect in the lives of our friends, coworkers, neighbors, etc., which will in turn flow out to their spheres of influence.

As we put mountains under our feet and pursue the land of freedom we were promised, we add to the weight of the influence of the gospel on earth.

I have battled a lot of things in my life, and I've had many reasons to camp on the wrong side of the mountain. And yet during those valley times, I spent much time with the Lord. And every time I got quiet in prayer and bent my ear toward heaven, I sensed the Lord say, *"You're made for better things than this. Please don't live like a pauper when I've made you royalty. I've put dreams in your heart, gifts in your spirit, and the capacity to greatly affect the world around you. Don't stay bound in doubt, self-hatred, and fear. Put that enemy under your feet and fight for all I've promised you!"*

Many mountains have passed under my feet since I heard those words: mountainous struggles with health, finances, relationships, neighborhoods, jobs, fear, anxiety, and on and on. Every powerful victory that has ever come to pass in my life has resulted from a tenacious, unflinching, "I-will-not-be-denied" kind of prayer.

The answers to these prayers have blessed me, yes. But more

than that, they've increased my capacity to minister in faith and to function as one who helps secure freedom for others. God wants to bless us with an abundant life because He loves us *and* because He expects that we will carry on the work of bringing His kingdom to earth. Be a wife of much prayer! Be a woman of prayer, one who conquers much for the kingdom of God!

As we venture to the higher places and determine to possess what God has promised, we will most certainly be opposed. We will have to get past roadblocks, understand strategy, and learn persistence. *I shall not be moved*

ROADBLOCKS AND LIFE KILLERS

"Listen to me! You can pray for anything, and if you believe, you will have it. But when you are praying, first forgive anyone you are holding a grudge against, so that your Father in heaven will forgive your sins, too" (Mark 11:24–25 NLT). What a promise from the most powerful force in the universe! We can pray for anything, and if we believe, we will have it. What are you aching to see come to pass in your marriage, in your world?

Now the tough question: Who do you need to forgive? Is it your husband? Are you holding an age-old account against him? When he messes up in a way that's consistent with past offenses, has he given you another rock to throw on the heap of judgment you have against him?

Or have you worked so hard at daily, ongoing forgiveness that when he does offend you in familiar ways, you see it as a stone to be acknowledged, then tossed in the river of forgetfulness? In other words, are you able to acknowledge his offense against you and then forgive him? Not that you have to be instantly "over it," but are you committed to the process of simply moving forward with a pure heart? This is not to say that you blindly trust him if he's not trustworthy. But can you forgive him and entrust yourself to God? Are you able to extend fresh mercies for present offenses because that's what's been extended to you?

Dear one, I know there are varying levels of offenses. I know some of you have wounds that go so deep you wonder if you'll ever fully heal from them. In that case, pray for God to provide you with a godly mentor who will gently lead you toward a place of restoration. God's healing and our forgiveness go hand in hand.

Some of you are dealing with repetitive offenses that cause you pain and frustration and require continual forgiveness. For years I battled the hot potato of unforgiveness. Just when I thought I had tossed the "potato" in the air for the last time, my dear husband would re-offend me in a familiar way. I'd find the potato in my hand once again, and each time it was a little bigger.

I knew freedom wouldn't happen without forgiveness. Since I wanted freedom, I was determined to obey. I kept tossing up that potato and declaring, "I forgive him, Lord, just as You've forgiven me! I will not hold this against him; I will bless him instead." Eventually the potato disappeared, leaving room in my hands to hold the grace that we both needed.

Forgiveness opens the door to fresh life, new beginnings, and everlasting impact. Forgiveness is hard work, but we must not underestimate its earthly and eternal significance. Unforgiveness, on the other hand, slams the door shut, stomps on the hope of new life, and keeps us from all of the good things God has promised us.

I imagine that unforgiveness has done more damage in the body of Christ than almost anything else. Unforgiveness between spouses has had repercussions such as ugly and uncomfortable silences in the home, bitterness, modeling unhealthy relationship patterns to children, rebellion in children, and has even been the source of physical ailments, depression, and suicide.

As entitled as we may feel to our list of offenses, that wretched list or account will kill the promise of an abundant present and a hopeful future. We need to forgive; we need to be forgiven; and we must be busy in prayer no matter on what side of forgiveness we find ourselves.

Jesus explained that if we don't forgive, neither does He. This declaration should make our hearts tremble. The minute you feel a speck of attitude toward *anyone*, cherish your connection with Jesus enough to get before Him and bless the person who has hurt or offended you.[1]

You've got much more important things to do in this world than to carry hot potatoes or manage a list of offenses! When you leave old offenses behind because you want all God has for you, all of heaven opens up before you. Now you're ready to reach up for the promises of God and make them a reality in your life.

STRATEGIES AND ROAD SIGNS

I'm not one for clichés, so I always find it funny when God speaks to my heart this way. During our one-sided season, I was pressing in hard for a breakthrough. My husband's company was a pressure cooker to work for, which only fueled his tendency to overwork.

I would not let up. The more I prayed, the more my faith grew that the breakthrough was at hand. But one day during my time of prayer, the Lord spoke a cliché-like phrase to my heart. I'm almost embarrassed to share it with you, but inside its goofy exterior is a profound word. Here goes: *Don't pray and peek; pray and seek.*

Are you still with me? As I sat there awhile praying and paging through Scripture, this is the correction that was made clear to me. Don't fold your hands, pray your prayers, and then *peek* over your hands for the slightest sign that there's finally money in the checkbook, or that your husband is finally reading the Bible, or that his demanding job is about to change. When we begin peeking for "signs" of the answers to prayer we expect, we place ourselves at risk of being led astray, being deceived, and turning our faith-walk into one rabbit chase after another. If God wants to give us a sign, we'll know it. In fact, He's already put countless signs in place for our benefit and direction. Really, they're everywhere.

Hanging on the stars in the night sky is a sign that says, "Tomorrow is another chance to begin again." Rising with the sun are signs that say, "New mercies are waiting at your door" and "The lovingkindness of the Lord is new each morning." The birds carry a banner that says, "Your Father knows all about you and cares about every detail." The trees that stretch toward the heavens display a sign that says, "You were made to worship Him." And on the cross hangs a sign that says, "You were worth dying for. Resurrection power is now available to redeem every part of your life!"

God knows our needs, and if we need a token of our faith or a reminder that He is very much at work, He will show it to us. So when we pray, we must not assess the quality or success of our prayers by constantly "peeking" and overanalyzing the object of our prayers. First we pray, and then we seek the Lord with all our hearts. We ask for gifts from His hand; in fact, we're told that every good gift comes from Him (see James 1:17). But more important than what He gives us or shows us is that we keep pressing on to know Him more.

Something wonderful happens when we pray and *seek*. Our requests take a backseat to having intimate fellowship with the One our soul loves. Not that the needs we've expressed in our prayers don't matter; but we find ourselves more assured that God cares even more about our well-being than we do.

We may start out pursuing Him to get what we want (and the Lord, in His kindness, does not turn us away); but the more we get to know *Him*, the more we count every lesser thing as rubbish. Still, as we delight in Him, He gives us the desires of our hearts (see Psalm 37:4). What an amazing, precious Lord we serve.

So pray, dear sister. And then climb your mountain in faith and expectation. Seek His face and rest in His love. It's the only way to go.

PERSISTENCE AND PROMISES

"Keep on asking, and you will be given what you ask for. Keep on looking, and you will find. Keep on knocking, and the door will be opened. For everyone who asks, receives. Everyone who seeks, finds. And the door is opened to everyone who knocks" (Matthew 7:7–8 NLT).

Journeying to our place of promise is hard work. We will have bumps in the road and battles along the way. Here's where tenacity comes into play. Do we want the promised life badly enough? Do we want stable marriages, hearts refreshed, and powerful prayers? Are we willing to go the distance with all that threatens what God has promised us?

I shudder when I imagine how many times I've been inches

away from laying hold of a promise only to give up in unbelief. How many times do you suppose we have persisted in prayer, looked around for evidences of God moving, and then abandoned our post because we thought that maybe God wasn't in it after all?

God loves us. He wants us free. He wants us healed and whole. Belief pleases Him. Unbelief tires and angers Him. Read the Gospels. Over and over again you'll see accounts of unbelief that caused Jesus to stop and question if anyone had been paying attention or learning from the things they'd just seen. And when He did come across someone with great faith, Jesus made it a point to let everyone know. He paid for it, and now He wants us to walk in the freedom He provided for us. All of God's promises are yes and amen! "For every one of God's promises is 'Yes' in Him. Therefore the 'Amen' is also through Him for God's glory through us" (2 Corinthians 1:20 HCSB).

We don't have to wonder if it's God's will to bless us—it is! We don't have to wonder if it's God's will to restore and heal us—it is! We don't have to wonder if God wants our husbands to be powerful, spiritual leaders of our homes—He does!

We must pray from a place of triumph because victory has been won in the spiritual realm. But we need to walk out these promises on earth with persistent prayer and ferocious faith. If we do this and do not let up, things around us *will* start to change.

No doubt you have bumps in your road and mountains casting shadows over you, but do not relent! You are in a strategic position to pray for life-changing blessings into your marriage and your family and your world! This is the battle worth fighting. *Things* change when you pray. *You'll* change when you pray. Pray all day, every day, or as often as you think of it.

SPIRITUAL LIFT:

"Heaven is open to you; the treasure and powers of the world of the spirit are placed at your disposal on behalf of those around you. Learn to pray in the name of Jesus."

□ *Andrew Murray*[2]

LENDING A HAND

Watch Your Step—Be careful not to confuse resilient prayer with repetitious prayer. One is motivated by passion, the other, performance. God is not interested in repetitive words if our hearts are not engaged. Keep your mind and heart engaged in what you are saying. Fan the flame and keep your prayer life alive.

Stay on the Right Path—Remember to spend some time just resting and delighting in the Lord. And in order to thrive in your relationship with God, communication must go both ways. Be quiet and listen to what He has to say. Find a verse that speaks to your mountain and write a personalized prayer around it. Pray out loud, and your faith will grow. Remember to pray for others as often as you pray for yourself. Consider your time of intercession one of the most powerful things you can do.

Run From—Run from all of the time wasters that rob you of your time in prayer. Ask God to show you if some other things have to go or be put on hold for a season so you can tend to what's going on in your marriage.

Destination Ahead—Run toward the promises of God! Remember, God's promises are "yes" to you! Take Him at His word and put one foot in front of the other. On your weary and bored days, remind yourself that you're almost there.

Watch the Fine Line—While God longs to bless us and provide for us, He is not our divine vending machine, nor is He our servant. We are His and we must follow wherever He leads. Sometimes He asks us to run when we'd rather rest and rest when we'd rather run. He gets to decide. We walk the fine line by embracing a holy expectation that God will be big in our midst and a humble understanding that we will follow Him always and anywhere.

God's Promise for You Today—"Ask of Me, and I will make the nations Your inheritance and the ends of the earth Your possession" (Psalm 2:8 HCSB).

Holy Father in heaven,

I am quite sure that I barely scratch the surface when it comes to pulling down Your promises and making them a reality on earth. So, Lord, I ask for a supernatural vision of what You want to do around me. And I ask for divine faith to lay hold of it. Fuel my prayer life so that I'm a force with which to be reckoned! I am not on this earth or in this marriage to suffer one defeat after another. You've appointed me for exploits for such a time as this. Holy is Your name. May Your kingdom

*come to earth, and may Your kingdom come to the marriages
in my community. Amen.*

TO THINK ABOUT...

1. Read Psalm 145:18–20

a. According to verse 18, what component is necessary in
order for the Lord to hear us when we pray?

b. What four things are promised to the believer who
prays this way?

c. What a treasure it is to be cherished and so attentively
cared for by the most powerful force in the universe.
Write a prayer thanking God for His promise to love and
watch over you.

2. Read Matthew 7:7–8

a. Can you think of a time when you persisted in prayer
for something until the victory came? Explain.

b. Is there something you've stopped praying for because
you simply lost hope? Describe. Now read the verse
above again. How is God speaking to you in regard to
this desire of your heart? Write it down.

c. With a prayerful heart, consider this verse again, and
write down a prayer for your marriage. Record this
prayer also on an index card in your Bible; tuck it in the
book of Matthew on the page of chapter 8, verses 7 and
8. Begin your persistent prayer, and when you get weary,
read the passage from Matthew again.

3. Read Matthew 7:9–12

a. Using verses 9 through 11, write a personalized, paraphrased prayer that tells of the goodness of God and of His desire to give good gifts to His children. Make it personal about the longings of your heart and God's great desires for you.

b. Verse 12 may seem out of place in a passage on prayer, but it's very much in place. Since we've been given these great and precious promises of fellowship with God and answered prayer, we are to do in faith for others what we would want done for us. Our capacity to be a huge blessing to others is exponentially increased when we understand that God is just waiting to answer prayers that line up with His will. I pray that your listening prayer time will be an especially sweet time for you. Your only guideline is this: What does God want to tell you about all of the magnificent ways He wants to use you? Enjoy.

4. Try a different approach in your prayers this week. If you don't usually kneel, spend some time on your knees. If you don't raise your hands, try it once. Pray out loud if you usually pray quietly. Put on instrumental music if you're used to silence. Be silent if you've never done that before. The purpose of this exercise is to help you keep things fresh. But the most important component of prayer is presence. Show up, be engaged, and ask the Holy Spirit to guide you as you pray. Pray for your husband. Pray for your marriage. Pray for your church. Pray for your country. Pray for your persecuted brothers and sisters around the world. No matter what, every chance you get, pray.

Twelve

FAITH, HOPE, AND LOVE

*May you experience the love of Christ, though it is so
great you will never fully understand it. Then you
will be filled with the fullness of life and power that
comes from God. Now glory be to God! By his mighty
power at work within us, he is able to accomplish
infinitely more than we would ever dare to ask or hope.*

□ Ephesians 3:19–20 NLT

FAITH . . .

I WAS CLEANING the house one spring day
when I looked out the window and saw my youngest son sitting in a
lawn chair at the end of the driveway. The wind was blowing hard, so
I grabbed a jacket and went out to talk to my little boy.

He looked up at me with a smile and stated, "I'm having a
garage sale like you did last week." "A garage sale?" I asked. "Just
what are you selling?" He pointed underneath his chair to a fire
truck.

I asked, "How are people supposed to know you're selling the
truck that's sitting under your chair, honey?" His dimpled smile
undid me when he pointed to a sign he made.

The sign had a few problems, though. You couldn't really read it. And even more troubling was that he taped it to the edge of the chair where his legs hung down, which really wasn't the greatest problem, because the wind slapped the sign up against the bottom of the chair and kept it there.

No one would know about Jordan's "garage sale," and I knew he would be sitting outside for a long time. Yet he was so proud of his ingenuity and he was ready to wait for his buyer. I thought of making a few helpful suggestions, but he was perfectly happy with his effort.

I kissed him on the top of the head and went back inside. I kept a mother's eye on him and my heart melted every time a car whizzed by without so much as a look. Finally, I could take it no longer and I went out there with a five-dollar bill. "I'll buy your truck, honey."

Jordan's dimples appeared again and he hopped down from his chair. He bent down, picked up the truck, and handed it to me. He took the money and with only sweetness said, "Thanks, Mom."

You know, it's like that with God. When we take our imperfect selves and resources and move out to a place of childlike faith and expectation, God can barely contain Himself. He has to move. Faith means everything to God. He isn't put off by our fumbling efforts; He is completely captivated by our belief.

Where is your expectation level? With regard to your husband, your marriage, and your sphere of influence, what mountains are you expecting God to move? As we touched on in the last chapter, unbelief angers God; but belief, well, that makes His heart swell!

And it's not enough to "put our truck at the end of the drive-way." We have to show up too. Our whole mind, body, soul, and spirit must be engaged in this pursuit of God and this walk of faith.

(The following story is my husband's. As I mentioned on the dedication page and in the acknowledgments, Kevin has carried me more miles than I've ever carried him. He was generous to allow me to write this book and share some of our struggles.)

My one-sided season . . . wow, I'm not sure where to start. You see, I don't really think that way; I am someone who generally just does what needs to be done. At first glance that may sound sort of noble, but it actually has more to do with a heart that deep inside believed I could do it best by myself. In some ways that attitude has served me well; I tend to accomplish a lot. It has also hurt me in ways I don't often talk about out loud.

As I recall, my faith was rarely exercised while growing up; that muscle was weak. When I married Susie, my true love, and started my family, God had a plan to deal with my way of thinking. Ironically that plan involved me having to do a lot, from holding a job or two, taking care of our young kids and household, and caring for my wife during a long-term illness. I did my best by relying on the physical muscles that had been developed over the years, but God was trying to break my dependence upon myself. He wanted me to learn to use spiritual muscles of faith in Him that had been somewhat neglected.

I remember feeling like I had too many plates spinning at once. Many days I just had to go to work but knew my family desperately needed me too. It was very hard for me to leave Susie at home day after day with our three active little boys knowing that she could not physically get up to care for them. The hardest mornings were the ones when I had to peel Susie's tearstained hands off of mine so I could go to work.

I remember wondering each day if this would be the day that something really bad would happen to the kids while I was gone, or if this would be the day that Susie's health would take a turn for the worse. I couldn't be in two places at once.

I was forced to choose between caring for my family financially by going to work and caring for them physically by staying home. I knew I couldn't do both, and I remember feeling like I wasn't doing a very good job at either. That season culminated with me being diagnosed with cancer. God was after my dependence. If and when we will yield to Him, God gets what He is after.

As I look back on the seasons God has brought us through, I can see that His ways are higher than my ways and His wisdom is greater than my wisdom.

While I still fight with God at times and don't always understand what He is up to, I trust Him now. I know that His number one goal is to develop our dependence so that our first response is to call on Him through difficult times. I can't imagine a more effective way that God could have dealt with my overdependence on self than to make me try to do it by myself. While I wouldn't wish a one-sided season again on myself or anyone else, I wouldn't trade mine for anything either.

—Kevin Larson

Let me ask you—when you show up to your prayer time and you cry out to the Lord, do you open your hands in expectation because you *know* He will act on your behalf? Can you fit your expectation in a thimble or a cup or a bucket? Are you looking for momentary relief or a radical transformation of your life?

Every morning when I show up for my quiet time, I put out seven buckets of expectation before the Lord. I am asking Him to be big in my boys' lives (and those of their future wives); I am asking Him to do huge things in my church; I am asking God to give Kevin and me an increased capacity for His presence and His Word; and I pray as well about a number of other things. Everything I am asking for is biblical and is God's expressed will for His people, so I know that these prayers are pleasing to Him.

Have you ever considered this? Those who believe that miracles were for long ago and not for today are limited to receiving only as they believe. Miracles happen where faith is present.

The truth of Scripture is as relevant now as it has been for all the ages. And Jesus said, "*Anything* is possible if you will only believe" (see Mark 9:23). Amazingly, God responds more to faith than He does to need.

Just the other day during my prayer time, this verse jumped out at me:

> In my anguish I cried to the LORD, and he answered by setting me free. (Psalm 118:5 NIV)

We cry for relief but He answers by giving us freedom. We might ask for a change of clothes and a fresh meal while we're in prison, and He answers by opening the prison doors! We ask for a break and He gives a breakthrough. Jesus says to us, "I'm not interested in making life easier for you if it keeps you in bondage. I'm after your freedom, and you should be too!"

How do we lay hold of this, you ask? We ask! We ask God to

increase our faith. We ask Him to increase our husband's faith. We ask Him to make our path so clear that it's impossible for us to miss. We ask Him to use this season of life to strengthen our relationships with our children. And if we have any expectancy in us, let's wrap it around our prayers and bring them before the Lord. We must dare to believe that we are making a powerful difference in our marriages, our personal lives, and the lives of our children, because when we add expectancy to our prayers, we are.

It's okay if our questions are small, as long as we plant a seed of faith every time we pray. *Every time*, Jesus moves on our faith, and *every time*, He more than makes up where we are lacking. Dear one, don't worry if your eyes don't see movement *every* time you pray. Don't be concerned if you sometimes *feel* nothing when you pray. That's where faith comes in. What kind of faith would be required if we got everything we wanted right when we asked for it? Worse yet, what kind of women would we be? Character is built through delays, hardships, and waiting. But we don't have to stay stuck there. And the Word says that every time we pray, He hears us.

God is always listening, always moving, always working on our behalf. In fact, this very day you are experiencing or walking amidst answers to prayers that were prayed on your behalf a long time ago.

Someone prayed for your walk of faith, or your perspective, or that you would be provided for. You asked God to speak to you, or bless your children, or help you with something at work, and He did. All too often we assign blame to God for not answering our prayers when He did in fact answer them, just not how or when we wanted Him to.

In spite of this misunderstanding, God listens to our prayers, and lovingly and continually moves hearts and circumstances so that we will be blessed. God works on our behalf and we wonder why He isn't moving quicker. We don't see what God is up to, so we clench our fists and stomp our feet while standing on the new kitchen floor we prayed for last year.

At some point we have to settle the issue that God is good and He wants to bless our lives more than we can imagine.

In the last chapter I mentioned that unforgiveness has done more damage in marriages and in the body of Christ than almost anything else. Well, I must say I think the sin of unbelief has to be right up there with unforgiveness at the top of the list of things that can damage a marriage.

What would happen if a revival of faith broke out in Christian marriages everywhere? Can you imagine the lives that would be transformed? Finances, lovemaking, time commitments, and relationships all renewed, redeemed, and brought into a holy balance. What a powerful thought. And this is surely something God wants to do!

My life verse is Psalm 116:9 and says, "And so I walk in the Lord's presence as I live here on earth!" The Lord's presence heals, nourishes, renews, and restores. The Lord's presence is bursting with promise. Interchange the word *promise* with *presence* and read the verse again. *And so I walk in the Lord's promise as I live here on earth.* This is our heritage in the family of faith, dear sister.

Our faith in what God will do says everything about who we think God is. And He is good and strong and loving. He has given us access to the heavenly realm not only for eternity, but for today and for tomorrow and for next week. How amazing it is that we are willing to be such earthbound travelers when Jesus has willingly linked us together with Himself. We're not here to just get by. We're here to thrive and grow and abound in every good work!

We can love God and be afraid. But we cannot please Him without faith. On the other hand, He greatly rewards those who have the courage to show up and believe Him for better things. Dear sister, let's hold unswervingly to the hope we profess, because the One we're hoping in is so very faithful.[1]

Miracles happen when you walk in faith.

HOPE . . .

"What is faith? It is the confident assurance that what we hope for is going to happen. It is the evidence of things we cannot yet see" (Hebrews 11:1 NLT).

What is hope? It's the thing that compels us to continue on because we know something better lies ahead. Hope makes us hang in there when we feel like quitting. Hope keeps us watching for a breakthrough even when our eyes are tired. Hope challenges us to remember that God is good and that He rewards those who hold tenaciously to His promises.

Our hopes are often dashed when our view is restricted. We lose hope when we only see what is in front of us: our ability, our circumstances, our earthly world, and ourselves. Hope is renewed, though, when we set aside the possibility that we can change our situation in our own strength and once again, over and over, put our eyes on Jesus.[2]

How willing we are to camp on the wrong side of the mountain and forfeit the life God has promised us! We must go on a frantic search for God and His promises. We must look for Him until we find Him; and when we find Him, we must never let Him go! The more desperate the situation, the more desperate the search! Blessed are we who earnestly search for God, because He *will* be found by us.

—×—

God designed marriage to be a reflection of Christ's relationship with the church. Both the church and marriage are under attack today. The Devil wants to undermine and minimize marriage and make a mockery of the church because these things are sacred to God. Anything he can do to mock what is important to God, he will do. That's why our holiness and response to difficult seasons is so incredibly important in the whole scheme of things.

Our churches and communities are either strengthened or weakened by whether or not we choose hope when things feel hopeless. Hope is our rope; it's our way out of the deep caverns we fall into as we journey along the way. We don't hope in our husbands. We love our husbands and hope in God.

Bring a godly hope to your marriage. Understand that a revival in your home will affect generations of tomorrow. Who knows what seeds have been planted on your behalf? Others are praying for you; I am praying for you, and most important, Jesus, the *hope* of the world, is interceding for you day and night, and He promises never to quench the smallest hope (see Isaiah 42:3; Matthew 12:20). You have every reason to hope, and hope does not disappoint. [3]

Miracles happen when you walk in hope.

LOVE . . .

Once during a time of prayer, I began meditating on certain passages of Scripture that described the final hours of Christ's life. I couldn't help but wonder what it must have been like for the angels. And though this story is purely speculative on my part, I ask you to take a moment and imagine Christ's journey from *the angels' perspective*. . . .

The angels watched in horror as their brave King stumbled up the hill to the place where He would be executed. How could this be happening? They remembered the day He stood up from His throne and informed the heavenly hosts of His journey to earth, His journey to live as a man. Did He have to go? Did He have to lower Himself to their level, just to reach them? Were they worth it? Will they understand? Will they care? "Some will, and some will not," was His reply.

But with all of their questioning, the angels knew the answer. He loved His creation, He watched over them, and He would do what He needed to in order to save them.

Now all they could do was to wait for one word from Him, and they would gladly rescue Him from this wretched scene. The soldiers roughly turned Jesus around before laying Him on the splintered cross. Jesus looked with mercy at a soldier, and the soldier looked quickly away.

The angels held their breath as they caught a glimpse of His mangled back. In spite of the swelling and bruising, new blood still seeped from the open wounds and mixed with the old, sticky blood. Jesus winced as they lay Him on the splintered cross.

Never before had the angels felt so helpless, so wanting to intervene; they were at His beck and call, but He was not calling for them. He was going to do it. He was going all the way for His people.

The executioners still didn't know who it was that they had in their presence. They had in their midst a King, and not a tyrannical leader either; He was a humble Servant-King.

The sadness overwhelmed the angels. All of heaven wept as Jesus endured the torturous execution of a guilty man. People jeered, sneered, and spit at Him; and He opened not His mouth, except to pray for them.

Jesus felt the heaviness—the weight and the guilt of the prostitute and the pedophile. He endured the condemnation of the adulterer and the cheater. He wore the label of the idiot and the insecure. He paid for the sins of the critical wife and the overbearing husband.

For every person who would ever choose Him—He stayed there for them. He even felt the pain and stress from the times we have exaggerated, gossiped, and chosen selfishness over servanthood.

He felt it all and endured it all, all for the sake of love.

―――※―――

Love is the highest order of the day.

We were made for love. And when we look too long at ourselves or our spouses, we despair, because instead of love, we find selfishness there. But when we look to the Lord, we see something different. We see a Servant-King, one who depleted Himself that we might be filled. He didn't fight back. He didn't grab for His rights; He laid Himself down for love.

Jesus' example reminds us that the more pure the love, the more powerful the life. For years I wondered how a selfish person was supposed to love unselfishly. And it wasn't until I began spending more time trusting in *His* unfailing love than I did despairing over my unfailing selfishness that my life began to change.

Of course I loved the lovable and was good to those around

me. I was even able to make the loving choice or do the loving thing, but it wasn't always instinctive or fueled by a higher perspective. However, when I began immersing myself—every single day—in the knowledge that I am the object of God's great love, I actually became more loving!

You see, God's love heals and restores and builds up. And as I began *trusting* that God's whole posture toward me was one of deep love and affection—my capacity for love greatly increased. Compassion began spilling out of me, mercy was no longer a last resort, and forgiveness came quickly.

The Bible says, "I will *trust* in your *unfailing love*; my heart rejoices in your salvation. *I will sing* to the LORD, for he has been good to me."[4] How does this translate in our marriages and in our lives? It means we count on it, walk in it, rest in it, rely on it, operate from it, and get a vision and a hope for our relationships because of it. [5]

Read on: "Follow God's example in everything you do, because you are his dear children. Live a life filled with love for others, following the example of Christ, who loved you and gave himself as a sacrifice to take away your sins. And God was pleased, because that sacrifice was like sweet perfume to him" (Ephesians 5:1–2 NLT).

We are able to love because He loved us first. And when we walk in love, especially with the unlovable, God is overcome with joy. Every time we choose love over selfishness, we give Him a great return on His investment in us.

When the path gets long and the days drag on, and when you feel constantly irritated and critical of your husband, that's a perfect time to step off the mountain path, lie down in the grass, look up at the sky, and say out loud, "I'm so glad that You love me,

Lord! You cherish me and are pulling for me every single day. Because of Your great love, I can go anywhere and do anything You call me to do. And today, You've called me to love my family. Thank You for loving me, Lord."

Faith and hope are powerful life-transforming forces that will radically change our circumstances, and yet they are nothing without love. It doesn't matter if we've mastered a thousand languages or if we are the president of a big corporation; it doesn't matter what we've accomplished or how great the world thinks we are—we've missed the point if we've not walked in love. Everything of value, everything that will last beyond this life is born out of the commandment to love the way we've been loved. Love will change us, heal others, and fix what's broken. If we do nothing else today, let's be sure we love. Because, dear one, we are, and have been, and always will be the object of God's priceless love.

Let the storms come. As long as we hang on to the Lord, who is love, the storms will not take us off course. Through hardship and misunderstanding, over obstacles and mountains, victory is ours because we belong to Jesus; and He's not letting go of us.

Think about your journey for a moment. Now read this passage of Scripture with fresh eyes. See yourself as the victor you are. You are held, loved, guided, and protected. The Lord's watchful eye is on you, and nothing can separate you from His love.

"What shall we say about such wonderful things as these? If God is for us, who can ever be against us? Since he did not spare even his own Son but gave him up for us all, won't he also give us everything else? Who dares accuse us whom God has chosen for his own? No one—for God himself has given us right standing

□

with himself. Who then will condemn us? No one—for Christ Jesus died for us and was raised to life for us, and he is sitting in the place of honor at God's right hand, pleading for us.

"Can anything ever separate us from Christ's love? Does it mean he no longer loves us if we have trouble or calamity, or are persecuted, or hungry, or destitute, or in danger, or threatened with death? (As the Scriptures say, 'For your sake we are killed every day; we are being slaughtered like sheep.') No, despite all these things, overwhelming victory is ours through Christ, who loved us.

"And I am convinced that nothing can ever separate us from God's love. Neither death nor life, neither angels nor demons, neither our fears for today nor our worries about tomorrow—not even the powers of hell can separate us from God's love. No power in the sky above or in the earth below—indeed, nothing in all creation will ever be able to separate us from the love of God that is revealed in Christ Jesus our Lord" (Romans 8:31–39).

⸻

What a journey we've had together! I pray that you will never stop climbing, never stop hoping, always keep the faith, and immerse yourself in love. You have everything you need to conquer the mountains and live a powerful life of godliness.

SPIRITUAL LIFT:

"God is going to come to us in this next season of time, and His love will be almost beyond our capacity to bear. It will be the stuff of dreams, an unimaginable, monumental, incredible, astonishing, marvelous, outrageous love. . . . This is a season of wonder for us, and we will have to learn to live like much-loved children."

□ *Graham Cooke*[6]

Never give up. We were made for this, and miracles happen when we walk in love.

LENDING A HAND

Watch Your Step—On the days when God seems far away and you can't even hear the faintest whisper of His voice, don't panic. Just rely on what you know to be true. You are loved, called, accepted, and equipped. No matter how you feel, God's Word is true for you.

Stay on the Right Path—Remember that you are the object of God's abundant, immeasurable love. And so is your husband. Ask God to give you eyes to see yourself (and your honey) through His eyes. Dwell on love; think about His love. Thank Him for His love.

Run From—Run from consuming thoughts about your circumstances, and the tendency to have only earthbound thoughts. Run from the temptation to love only those who deserve it in your eyes. There's no reward in that. Love everyone around you.

Destination Ahead—Run toward every opportunity to build yourself up in faith, stir yourself up in hope, and nourish yourself in love.

Watch the Fine Line—You were made to scale mountains, witness miracles, and go from strength to strength and victory to victory. But . . . you will also stumble and fall and blow it more times than you care to know. When you feel strongest, you're often most vulnerable; and when you feel weak, you'll often find surprising strength. Walk in the holy confidence that declares you were made for another world, but embrace the humble dependence that confesses your need for Jesus every hour.

God's Promise for You Today—"Dearest friends, you were always so careful to follow my instructions when I was with you. And now that I am away you must be even more careful to put into action God's saving work in your lives, obeying God with deep reverence and fear. For God is working in you, giving you the desire to obey him and the power to do what pleases him" (Philippians 2:12–13 NLT).

THIS ONE IS FOR YOU . . .

My Beloved Daughter,

You are My precious treasure. One look at you and My heart skips a beat! I am so proud of the way you earnestly pursue what is right. I am with you on this journey, and I promise that you will reap a harvest of blessing if you continue on, and do not give up. Stay in step with Me, and I will restore the years the locusts have eaten. Stay in tune with My voice, and I will lead you to the high places. Obey Me quickly, and I will answer your prayers in ways that overwhelm you.

When the days feel heavy, promise Me you'll sing and dance with Me. When your heart is broken, promise Me you'll spend time with Me so I can speak truth to you. When you're weary, I will carry you. I've got your hand and I will not let go. You have every reason to be everything I've created you to be. Be full of faith and walk on in love. I love you and I always will. Until we meet again . . .

Your Beloved Bridegroom

A FINAL WORD . . .

> *Be on your guard.*
> *Stand firm in the faith.*
> *Be women of courage.*
> *Be strong.*
> *Do everything in love.*
> ——SEE I CORINTHIANS 16:13–14

TO THINK ABOUT...

1. Read Hebrews 11:6

a. At some point we have to take the leap and jump into faith with both feet, trusting that God is who He says He is and that He will come through for us. This is about entrusting our whole selves—our dreams, our fears, our desires, and our inadequacies—to the One who loves us. We were made to please Him, and we need faith to do that. Start showing up to your quiet time with buckets of expectation. Take a moment now to label each "bucket" (e.g., a godly, thriving marriage, children who love God, a powerful prayer life, etc.).

b. Let this sink in for a moment: We get to come into God's presence anytime we want to! We don't have to get in line or take a number. Looking at the second part of verse 6, notice there is another incredible benefit we receive as His children, as ones who seek Him. Write it down along with your thoughts on God's incredible graciousness.

2. Read Romans 15:13

a. Why do you suppose joy and peace and trust are connected to hope? Write down your thoughts. Describe a time when you possessed these three amidst a trying circumstance when you should have been anything but joyful, peaceful, and trusting in God. How did you find your way to the center of that storm? Explain.

b. Are things different now? Have you forgotten or let go of certain principles of hope that held you way back when? How about now? What do you now know about hope that you didn't back then? Explain.

c. Let's look at the bucket analogy again. What happens when you pour more water into the bucket than it was made to hold? Now read Romans 15:13 again. Think of your life as a bucket when you think of this verse. May you be filled, that you may overflow. . . . What adjustments can you make in your day and in your perspective so that you can "catch" the hope that the Lord is offering you each day? Write these adjustments down and share them with your accountability partner. Guard your hope; it's your rope.

3. Read 8:31–39

a. I love this passage of Scripture! Choose either the whole passage or just a few verses and write out a bold, declarative personalized prayer. Overwhelming victory is yours, dear one.

b. Time for listening prayer. Use this same passage as your guideline and enjoy some time well spent with the Lord.

4. Take your Bible and go to a library, a coffee shop, or a quiet place in the house. Get out of your normal routine. If you have an iPod or a CD player, put some instrumental music on in the background. Open your Bible to 1 Corinthians 13. Spend some time meditating on this powerful chapter. Think about who you are and how far you've come. Imagine that you've been selected to speak at a friend's wedding shower. Your topic is love. Take time now and write your message, one you believe in.

Always be ready to give an account for the hope that is within you . . . (see 1 Peter 3:15).

ACKNOWLEDGMENTS

TO MY WONDERFUL agent, Beth Jusino: Thank you for holding on to the vision for this book. I appreciate you so very much. To Peg Short: Thank you for believing in what I do. To the staff at Moody: I love you all! Thanks for showing me such a great time in Chicago. To my editor, Pam Pugh: Thank you for encouraging me and for working hard on my behalf. I'm so glad you can be bribed with chocolate. Bless you, my friend.

Two years ago I enjoyed a chat with Mick Silva at the Mount Hermon Christian Writers Conference. This book was inspired during that visit. Thanks, Mick, for the time and encouragement.

Kay Blake, what can I say to you? Your love, support, prayers, and volunteer hours have kept me on the path of productivity. I love you dearly.

To my sample readers who shared their time, their stories, and their invaluable insights. Bless you, girls! Thank you Patty L., Linda A., Daryl J., Jeannie T., Cindy L., Tanda E., Shari C., Amy L., Tish I., Patty F., Peg K., Gail M., Cheryl S., Tammy R., Susan S., Julie H., Lori B., Mary Jo F., Cathy H., Amy Z., and the First Peter Wives Group of Twin Falls, Idaho. I would like to especially thank Bonnie, Judy, and Janet for holding up my arms, standing by my side, and helping me to bring this manuscript to its completion. Oh, how I love you all.

To the brave, godly women who shared their stories in this book: May your latter years be far more blessed than your former years! And may God fulfill His highest and best purpose for your lives!

To my three sons, Jake, Luke, and Jordan; you've grown into such fine young men. Your love for the Lord and your commitment to family blesses me beyond measure. May you change the world by the way you love your future wives. You are my treasures.

To my husband, Kevin, I love you. Your strength and tenderness make the love of Christ comprehensible to me. What a great sport you've been in allowing me to write this book! You even came up with your own title: *How to Carry the Load You Married.* You make me laugh. God has shown us what is possible for those who love, believe, and walk humbly with Him. Bless you, sweetie.

To Jesus, my one and only; You continue to amaze me. I want to give You a great return on Your investment in me. Glorify Your name, Lord. I love You most.

FINAL NOTE:

One million new children are trafficked into forced prostitution each year (UNICEF). International Justice Mission is a human rights organization that works to rescue these dear ones and bring just consequences under the law to the perpetrators. Over the past ten years, their lawyers, investigators, and social workers around the world have rescued thousands of victims of sex trafficking and other forms of abuse and oppression. The author is donating 25 percent of her royalties to support this cause.

NOTES

CHAPTER ONE

1. Strong boundaries are sometimes required in certain desperate situations. Be sure to seek godly counsel for your particular situation.

2. Francis Frangipane, *The Stronghold of God* (Lake Mary, FL: Charisma House, 1998), 32.

CHAPTER TWO

1. Linda Dillow, *Calm My Anxious Heart* (Colorado Springs: Nav-Press, 1998), 121.

2. A. W. Tozer, *The Pursuit of God* (Camp Hill, PA: Christian Publications, Inc., 1995), 145.

CHAPTER THREE

1. "Morning and Evening," Charles Spurgeon, Heartlight, Inc., 1996–2006, 8/24 entry.

CHAPTER FOUR

1. Quotes from brainyquotes.com.
2. Quote by Henry Ward Beecher from Heartlight.org.

CHAPTER FIVE

1. MAC Dictionary/Thesaurus Program.
2. See Romans 8:1.
3. From the article, "Your Appointment Awaits You," by Francis Frangipane (go to frangipane.org).
4. Pastor J. J. Slag serves on staff at Emmanuel Christian Center in Minneapolis, MN.
5. See Romans 8:37.
6. Mary W. Tileston, *Joy and Strength* (New York: Barnes & Noble, 1993), 187.
7. Ibid.
8. Some resources on this topic are *Fasting for a Spiritual Breakthrough* by Elmer Towns and *Hunger for God* by John Piper.

CHAPTER SIX

1. http://quotations.about.com/od/morepeople/a/teresa_quote2.htm.
2. Beth Moore, *When Godly People Do Ungodly Things* (Nashville: Broadman & Holman, 2002), 106–07.

CHAPTER SEVEN

1. See 2 Corinthians 12:9–10.
2. Graham Cooke, *The Language of Love* (Grand Rapids: Chosen Books, 2004), 45.
3. Mary W. Tileston, *Joy and Strength* (New York: Barnes & Noble, 1993), 206.

CHAPTER EIGHT

1. Francis Frangipane, taken from "In Christ's Image Training," Level One Audio Series, 2002 Arrow Publications, Inc., Cedar Rapids, IA.
2. See Isaiah 30:18; 64:4; and Lamentations 3:25.
3. Susie Larson.
4. Adapted from a story attributed to Alice Gray, http://www.atthewell.com/pearls/.
5. Susie Larson, *Balance That Works When Life Doesn't* (Eugene, OR: Harvest House, 2005), 120.

NOTES

☐

6. Andrew Murray, *Waiting on God* (Minneapolis: Bethany, 2001), 92.

CHAPTER NINE

1. See Numbers 11:1 and Proverbs 21:19.
2. See Psalm 139:5.
3. A. W. Tozer, *The Knowledge of the Holy* (New York: Harper & Row, 1961), 83.

CHAPTER TEN

1. "Jesus, What a Wonder You Are," by Dave Bolton.
2. For further study see Proverbs 11:11; 12:6; 18:21; and Luke 6:27–36.
3. Francis Frangipane, *The Stronghold of God* (Lake Mary, FL: Charisma House, 1998), 90.

CHAPTER ELEVEN

1. See Matthew 6:15 and Colossians 3:13.
2. Andrew Murray, *Believing Prayer* (Minneapolis: Bethany House, 1980), 55.

CHAPTER TWELVE

1. See Luke 18:6–8; Hebrews 10:23; 11:6.
2. This paragraph written by my friend Kay Blake.
3. See Romans 5:1–5.
4. See Psalm 13:5 (NIV).
5. See 1 John 4:16.
6. Graham Cooke, *The Language of Love* (Grand Rapids: Chosen Books, 2004), 66.

Lies Women Believe

And the Truth that Sets Them Free

In *Lies Women Believe*, Nancy Leigh
DeMoss exposes areas of deception she
believes are common to Christian
women and are at the root of their
struggles. Some of the lies include lies
about God, sin, priorities, marriage,
family, and emotions. She deals
honestly with women's delusions and il-
lusions and then gently leads them to
the truth of God's Word that leads to
true freedom.

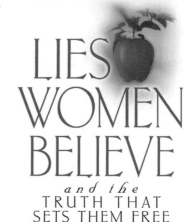

ISBN-10: 0-8024-7296-6
ISBN-13: 978-0-8024-7296-0

The Companion Guide
for Lies Women Believe

*A Life-Changing Study
for Individuals and Groups*

Now here is a resource that will help
you go deeper with the truths from
Nancy's best-selling book *Lies Women Believe*. These penetrating questions will
make you and your friends think and
wrestle with the Truth as you search the
Word for answers to tough issues. Truth
is not just something to know but something to live out in the laboratory of life
as you apply the Word to real-life situations. *The Companion Guide for Lies Women
Believe* is ideal for small groups, Bible
studies, or Sunday school classes.

Previously titled *Walking in the Truth*.

ISBN-10: 0-8024-4693-0
ISBN-13: 978-0-8024-4693-0